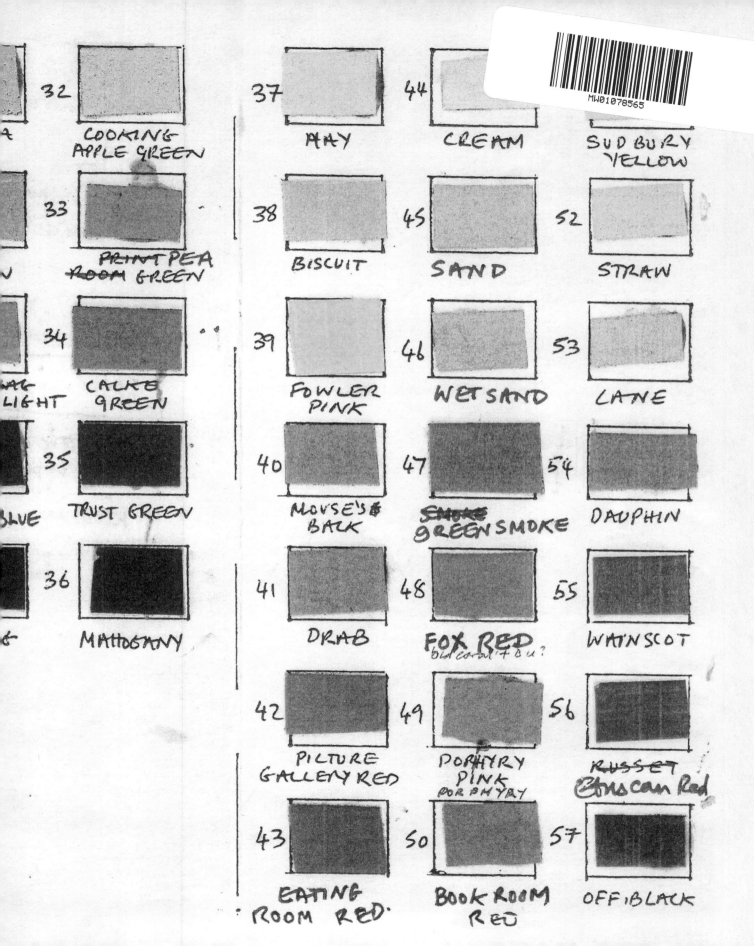

32 COOKING APPLE GREEN

33 ~~PRINT PEA~~ ROOM GREEN

34 CALKE GREEN

35 TRUST GREEN

36 MAHOGANY

37 HAY

38 BISCUIT

39 FOWLER PINK

40 MOUSE'S BACK

41 DRAB

42 PICTURE GALLERY RED

43 EATING ROOM RED.

44 CREAM

45 SAND

46 WET SAND

47 ~~SMOKE~~ GREEN SMOKE

48 FOX RED
Old Coral + B.u?

49 PORPHYRY PINK
PORPHYRY

50 BOOK ROOM RED

52 STRAW

53 LANE

54 DAUPHIN

55 WAINSCOT

56 RUSSET
Tuscan Red

57 OFF BLACK

44 SUDBURY YELLOW

THIS PAGE
Over the last few years, warm, earthy colours, such as Templeton Pink, have become increasingly popular, helping to make our homes into sanctuaries.

OVERLEAF
All the supposed rules about painting walls have disappeared, and a myriad of different ways of using colour are now being embraced in the home. Here, we see Whirlybird on the walls, with a border of stronger Bancha for a striking, modern look.

FARROW&BALL®

HOW TO REDECORATE

JOA STUDHOLME & CHARLOTTE COSBY

MITCHELL BEAZLEY

INTRODUCTION

Little did I know when I sat down to write the introduction to *How to Decorate* in 2015 that, all these years later, I would be doing it all over again for this brand new, updated version of the original: *How to Redecorate*. Much has changed in the way we treat our homes in the last decade; colour has been embraced with a vigour that has surprised us all, and this book reflects those changes while celebrating all things Farrow & Ball.

Decorating your home should be joyful. Without doubt, the most important thing is to use colours that you really love and feel comfortable with – there are certainly no fixed rules, so the ideas in this book are here not so much to influence, but to inspire, and to help you bring your vision to life.

Although founded more than 75 years ago, Farrow & Ball only opened its first showroom in London in 1996, when I was lucky enough to join the company after a decade making TV commercials. I had no formal training; I am Farrow & Ball home-grown, as is my colleague Charlotte Cosby, who is now the Creative Director, and it was our combined passion for all things colour that led us to conceive the idea of the original *How to Decorate* book.

I have worked with Farrow & Ball as their Colour Curator for more than 25 years and am immersed in the world of colour. A lot of my time is spent in people's homes showing them how colour can bring something special to their lives – amazingly, someone worked out that, on average, I decorate almost 5,000 rooms a year. I am also immensely privileged – and proud – to have the task of creating and naming new colours. Of course, these colours are the centre of our world, but their names have become equally iconic, so in this book we share some insight into the thinking that goes on behind the development of the colours and what we call them.

When it comes to paint colour, Farrow & Ball is the original and the best – our paint has a very particular look and it is one that simply cannot be copied. The extraordinary levels of high-quality pigment used in our paints result in a finish that is almost like velvet. It's a finish that you want to dive into, and with a depth of colour that is unsurpassed. These traditional values sit happily alongside more modern concerns about the environment, so I feel proud that all our products are water-based, low-odour and made using wind and solar power, and that our paints come in durable finishes that are perfect to cope with the rough and tumble of the modern home.

And just as we have developed as a company, we also believe that our palette has evolved to reflect the way we choose to decorate now. In the last few years, we have asked so much more of our homes, making them work harder to enhance the way we live. Many of us feel the need to create personal havens as a backdrop to our individual way of life. Often the solution to this can be found in the power of colour – creating different moods according to our own personal tastes, as well as separating our working hours from those of relaxation.

Some of us may still focus on our well-being by using layers of easy-to-live-with neutrals, which are all covered in this book, but increasingly we are attracted to the colours outlined over the next few chapters, to create a tingle of excitement mixed in with our own personal memories.

Although the bones of this book are much the same as the original – detailed advice on how to approach every architectural element in your home, including the thorny subjects of how to treat ceilings and floors, and how to make the most of the natural light – you will see that overall there has been a seismic shift in our approach to colour and the way that we use it. Warmer, kinder colours have gained in popularity over the cooler, greyer tones so beloved in the last decade. We now want colour to create lasting experiences in our homes, using it in umpteen quirky ways to reflect a little more of our personality. These are showcased in the new 'Transform Space with Colour' chapter, where you will see

THIS PAGE
This portrait of Charlotte
and me was taken in the paint
factory, where all the magic
happens. I can't tell you how
much we love it in there!

FACING PAGE

Our enduring relationship
with darks is shown at its
very best here, with Railings
on the units and De Nimes on
the walls. Using a darker
colour below the eye line
means the room opens out
in spite of it being such
a strong colour.

RIGHT

What could be more joyful
than these rooms with
their walls in Hegemone
wallpaper in different
colourways: Purbeck Stone
and Cornforth White (BP 5701)
in the foreground, and an
archived colourway beyond.
It makes for unusual but
very effective decorating.

eclectic mixes of colours, used to evoke the warmth and harmony of a more innocent age, and summed up by a growing trend for using friendly combinations of block colour.

My intention, as ever, is that you can use this book as a manual to refer to when you have a decorating quandary, but also when you simply need some inspiration. I have included some indispensable practical tools in the form of decorating tips and the three basic ways of combining colours, alongside some favourite personal colour combinations – I just couldn't resist.

Colour and pattern give rooms an extraordinary ambience and serve to remind us that our homes are not only incredibly special but also a celebration of our individuality. Over the last few years, we have recognized that thankfully we all like different things and that beauty continues to be very much in the eye of the beholder. This is reflected in the many different homes featured in this book, and I am indebted to those who have allowed us to celebrate them here. Despite their differences in size, date and style, the same basic principles apply to all. It is these principles that form the backbone of this book, and will hopefully help to turn your ideas and dreams into reality.

At Farrow & Ball, we are fiercely proud that, although our roots are firmly in the past, our palette is a constantly evolving collection of colours and patterns, rediscovered and reinvigorated for an ever-changing modern audience. Nothing gives us more joy than bringing colour into people's lives.

THE FARROW & BALL STORY

Farrow & Ball has deep roots. The company was founded in 1946 by John Farrow, an industrial chemist, and Richard Ball, an engineer, who had recently returned from Germany, where he had been a prisoner of war. Fortuitously, the two met when they both worked at a clay pit in Dorset. Together with their wives Peggy and Ena Rose, they then went on to establish their first paint factory in Verwood, also in Dorset, which supplied paint to the Admiralty and the War Office. In the 1960s, Farrow & Ball moved to Uddens Estate, near Wimborne, where it still is today, decades later.

During the 1970s and '80s, the company continued to expand, but while other paint manufacturers started to create acrylic paints containing more plastic and less pigment, Farrow & Ball continued using its original formulations, the finest ingredients, rich pigments and traditional processes, to make really high-quality paint which was quite different from commercial brands. This was all done out of the limelight in the heart of Dorset, which helped the company retain its identity and heritage, both of which would prove to be important factors in making the company so successful in the years to come.

In the early 1990s, historical decorator Tom Helme was looking for a paint company that could match his exacting standards, but he was unable to find one. That is, until a chance discovery of a tin of Dead Flat led him to the then sleepy Farrow & Ball. Tom persuaded his friend Martin Ephson to join him and together they took over running the company.

FACING PAGE
A very old and much treasured original Farrow & Ball paint tin. It might look plain, but it contained the first of the magic.

FACING PAGE
A cornucopia of
Farrow & Ball riches,
going back to the very
beginning of the company.
To this day, rearranging
the colour card is one of
our favourite jobs, and
although we continue to
add new colours, we try
to keep to the spirit
of the original card.

The signature Farrow & Ball paints were born through Farrow & Ball working closely in the restoration of historic buildings and creating colours that were sympathetic to their age. Then suddenly, the company's locally based and trade clients were joined by an army of people interested in interior design, excited to buy paints that they could see looked different with their unsurpassed quality and depth of colour. The paint names and colours were now being talked about in revered tones all over the UK, and in 1996 our first flagship showroom opened on the Fulham Road, in London's Chelsea, with me working behind the till! This was followed in 1999 by the opening of the first overseas showroom in Toronto, Canada, which also still flourishes to this day.

Over the following years, Farrow & Ball continued to grow apace, opening showrooms worldwide. Each one is styled more like a lifestyle store than a typical paint store. Our aim is to create a magnet for people to peruse the now world-famous palette of 132 paint colours, as well as the handcrafted wallpapers in a spacious, peaceful environment, with colour experts on hand to help and advise. Every colour we have ever made is still available from our archive. Colours in the Archive Collection are marked with an (A) in this book (see also page 226).

Today, Farrow & Ball distributes to more than 65 countries worldwide and has 60 showrooms, where you can work out your decorating dreams. It is no longer a sleepy little Dorset company.

NAMES AND INSPIRATION

I fell under the Farrow & Ball spell for the first time when, in the early 1990s, a whole new topic of conversation began. People were chatting regularly about the richness of Mouse's Back or scrumptious Smoked Trout (A), along with the freshness of Cooking Apple Green. It quickly became evident that these were not the contents of a Bacchanalian feast but the names of a palette of paints that had suddenly taken the world by storm. The names were so intriguing that one's imagination ran wild trying to visualize the colours with which they were associated. Little did I know that this would become one of the most important facets of my career. The paint names are now as much a part of our colours as the shades themselves and still evoke much discussion: 'Can I really paint my kitchen in Sulking Room Pink?'; 'How can a colour called Wine Dark possibly be blue rather than red?' These names bring the colours to life and are inspired by so many surprising sources.

We are more than aware that the psychology of colour names is powerful. Many people might doubt the wisdom of calling a colour Dead Salmon, for example, but this name is actually derived from a painting bill found for the decorating of the library at Kedleston Hall, Derbyshire, in 1805. 'Salmon' is the colour, while 'Dead' refers to the completely matt paint finish rather than a deceased fish. There are many other names that emanate from the animal kingdom, ranging from the delicate tone of Cabbage White, named after the equally delicate butterfly, to the more robust, if

vaporous, Elephant's Breath and Mole's Breath, two of the most-discussed Farrow & Ball names. However, all the paint names are rooted in much more than quirkiness or attention-seeking. Setting Plaster, for example, is simply named after the blushing walls of newly plastered houses.

String is, of course, the colour of untreated twine and works in perfect combination with Cord, another type of twine. These colour and name associations are intentional, if a little esoteric. De Nimes, named after the French city where denim was woven originally, has now been joined by Selvedge, referencing the covered internal seams. Treron, the green alternative to Farrow & Ball favourite Pigeon, is just that: a green species of pigeon. Jitney, meanwhile, shares its name with the bus that whisks New Yorkers from the city to the sandy beaches of The Hamptons at the end of the day. It sits perfectly with Stirabout, named after the porridge given to children in Ireland as an uplifting start to the day.

As true colourists, we at Farrow & Ball often take inspiration from original pigments, some of which have a surprising history. India Yellow is famously named after the pigment collected from the urine of cows that have been given a special diet of mango leaves. The rather grim-sounding Arsenic makes reference to the pigment that, historically, was often used in green wallpapers. There is a theory that Napoleon Bonaparte may have been poisoned by the arsenic used in the decoration of his bathroom on St Helena, where he was held in exile. However, please let me reassure you, there is nothing poisonous in our Arsenic, nor in any of our other paints.

Occasionally, a paint name is born almost before the colour. Plummett was mixed following an afternoon spent fishing on the river. The colour of the lead weight on the fisherman's line was a thing of such beauty that it just begged to be added to the Farrow & Ball palette. Similarly, there was a deep desire to make a white that was almost gossamer in appearance – a white with very little

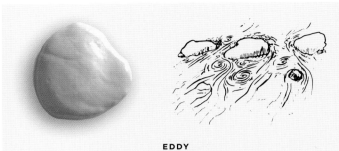

EDDY

Inspiration for recent colours and names have come from pastimes more prevalent during the coronavirus lockdown. Gentle green Eddy was named after the whirlpools favoured by wild water swimmers as natural Jacuzzis.

BEVERLY

This clean mid-green is named in honour of a kind and generous member of our Farrow & Ball team, who is sadly no longer with us. Like this classic colour, she was dependable and straightforward.

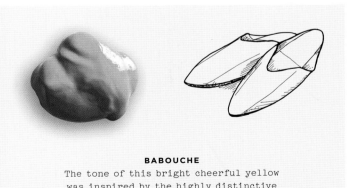

BABOUCHE

The tone of this bright cheerful yellow was inspired by the highly distinctive colour of the leather babouche slippers so often worn in Morocco.

TEMPLETON PINK

The historic feel of Templeton Pink took
its lead from the colour I used in the
renovation of the dining room in Templeton
House, a Georgian mansion in London that
was once the home of Winston Churchill.

KITTIWAKE

Cool clean blue Kittiwake takes
its name from the noisy seabirds
often seen on the Dorset coast
near Lulworth Cove, after which
a similar colour is named.

BAMBOOZLE

This spirited flame red is full of
buccaneering spirit and takes its name
from the word originally used to describe
the deceit of pirates when they ran the
wrong flag to trick other ships.

MATCHSTICK

This versatile and restrained tone needed
a name to match! It is inspired by the
unbleached wood used in the stalk of
a match — both the colour and the
object are equally understated.

HOPPER HEAD

Hopper Head, named after the iron containers used
to catch rainwater, sits directly between Farrow &
Ball classics Railings and Down Pipe — it definitely
needed a name associated with exterior ironmongery.

WHIRLYBIRD

Whirlybird takes its name from the
papery winged seeds that the young at
heart like to spin and were also the
inspiration for this upbeat colour.

FACING PAGE
The inner sanctum of the
Farrow & Ball project room,
the domain of the mighty
Shamus Pitts, whose
beautiful illustrations
of some of our colours are
depicted on the previous
pages. It is here that

showroom displays are born
and discussions of all things
colour take place.

additional colour and almost translucent – just like a spider's web. This was the birth of the colour Wevet, named after the Dorset dialect for exactly that: a spider's web.

Since Farrow & Ball has its roots firmly in Dorset, we have taken other paint names from the local dialect. Although not recognizable words, they are somehow so evocative that they bring the colour to mind anyway. Mizzle is named after the colour of the evening sky when there is a mix of mist and drizzle; Dimpse is quaint local dialect for the colour of the sky at twilight.

These colours are joined by another weather-related name, Cromarty, an area of sea off the northeast coast of Scotland, referred to in the BBC's daily radio broadcast of the *Shipping Forecast*, which warns sailors about impending gales. The name conjures up the colours of swirling mists and turbulent seas.

Nature will always be a great inspiration. Calluna, for example, is the colour, as well as the name, of the beautiful heather that brings late summer to life in the most rugged landscapes, while its stronger counterpart Brassica was inspired by the colour of the leaves of purple sprouting broccoli. I think it is obvious how iconic Pea Green (A) got its name!

Many of the Farrow & Ball colours have taken their cue from historic houses. Picture Gallery Red was inspired by the picture gallery at Attingham Park, Shropshire, while Sudbury Yellow is an interpretation of the decorator John Fowler's wall colour for the staircase at Sudbury Hall, Derbyshire. Calke Green is based on a cleaned version of the colour found in the breakfast room at Calke Abbey, also in Derbyshire. Inspiration for Cook's Blue came from there too, specifically the walls in the cook's closet, which had remained untouched for many decades. It is said that the colour was used to deter flies.

The tradition of looking to historic houses for colours endures to this day. Many of those that we create are based on surviving paintwork or on traditional colours handed down by successive generations of painters. Inchyra Blue was a bespoke colour I created for the classic Georgian Inchyra House in Perthshire. The colour needed to be sympathetic to the house's dramatic backdrop and work with the moody Scottish skies. Meanwhile, the lightest of our timeless neutrals, School House White, has its roots in a diminutive school house in the Somerset countryside.

A deserving lucky few have had colours named after them. Ball Green is a tribute to Richard Ball, the paint pioneer who founded the company with John Farrow, after whom Farrow's Cream is named. Savage Ground (A) owes its name to Dennis Savage, a block printer par excellence, who was instrumental in the creation of our very first wallpapers, while Sutcliffe Green (A) was named after John Sutcliffe, the revered colourist and co-creator of the signature Farrow & Ball colour card. He originally tried to pin words to colours to convey their 'essence', whether historically descriptive, exact (where pigment is involved) or even absurd, and it's a tradition I strive to maintain. The inspiration behind these colours are many, from my daughter's rosy cheeks to the works of Homer. How lucky we are to live in a world so full of glorious colour.

CREATING PAINT AND PAPER

There is a kind of alchemy that takes place during the creation of our paints, and that is why they look different. However, they often start life in the simplest of ways, usually at a kitchen table. Tens of ramekins filled with different shades are mixed and remixed for weeks on end until we are happy with the exact colour. They are then sent to the paint experts in our laboratory to be tested again.

Although we now make paint appropriate for every surface, Farrow & Ball was known originally for its specialist finishes, such as Dead Flat and Casein Distemper. Much was learned from the traditional production of these paints, which had very high levels of pigmentation, and now every finish from Farrow & Ball, ranging from Estate Emulsion to Full Gloss, has those same high levels of pigment, along with rich resin binders combined to create our signature depth of colour. The complex pigmentation produces uniquely interesting colours that have resonance and depth in their undertones. This causes them to change subtly in different light conditions, making them feel magical and alive. We use 12 exclusive pigments, all specifically selected for their colour intensity. By using these same pigments to make every colour in our palette, all our shades combine effortlessly, making it easy for you to put together a cohesive colour scheme.

Some people question the fact that Farrow & Ball paint is not thick, that it has the texture of single, or light, cream, rather than a jelly-like texture. Quite simply put, we make our paint quite differently and this less-viscous nature of the paint ensures that it flows well, to create an even surface. Every colour made is packed with lots of rich pigment, blended with enormous care and precision, and scrupulously tested in all lights before it even reaches the tin, because we believe that paint is more than just a veneer.

FACING PAGE
There is something delightfully artisan about our paint factory, where our dedicated and loyal staff take enormous pride in the paints they produce, constantly checking the quality and colour.

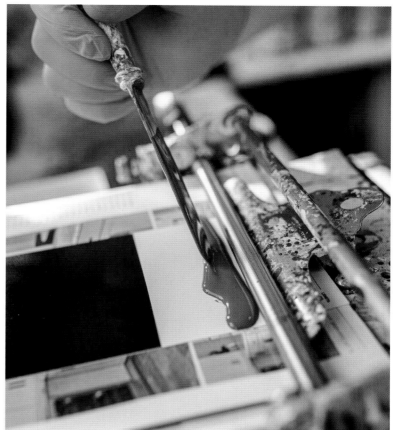

When it comes to making wallpaper, the same care and precision is put into practice. Throughout history, block-printed papers have always been treasured, but in recent times most of the paper produced in this way has been used purely in the restoration of historic houses. Although the Farrow & Ball method of making wallpaper was first introduced in the 18th century, it has luckily had a little help from the 21st.

Each wallpaper design is achieved by using a hand-brushing technique for applying the background colour, resulting in visible brush strokes, just as it would have done in the 18th century. The blocks for the patterns have Farrow & Ball paint applied to them, and these are then overlaid onto the paper. The use of our own paint increases the depth of colour and means that each part of the pattern is slightly proud. It also imparts a pleasing soft finish that cannot be emulated by printer's ink. Colour printed on top of colour produces remarkable effects, impossible by any other means, and creates a slight variation from one repeat to the next, making the papers feel even more like works of art.

Farrow & Ball has always been famous for its traditional stripes and drags, which are produced using the open-trough method. To achieve this, the roll of ground paper is passed slowly under paint-filled, open-bottom troughs to create the background colour, and then the paper is run through the machine a second time, but with some areas of the trough blocked off to create a continuous stripe.

In order to make these papers appropriate for the modern day, endless work has gone into ensuring that they have the same chalky finish that has always defined our paint colours, but now they are also wipeable, thereby combining timeless artistry with 21st-century durability.

FACING PAGE
The wallpaper factory is full of exciting treasures, from the meticulously made blocks and rollers to the basic but essential jugs, which are still used to introduce our paint to the ground paper.

PART ONE

—

WHERE TO START

FACING PAGE
I created School House
White for this very room.
It is seen here on the
walls and ceiling, paired
with Drop Cloth on the trim.
I also wrote much of this
book at the table.

Ceiling

Coving

Glazing Bars

Wall

Window Frame/Architrave

Dado Rail/Chair Rail

Panelling/Dado

Skirting

Floor

INTERIOR ARCHITECTURAL DETAIL

Ceiling Rose

Ceiling

Cornice

Frieze

Picture Rail

Doorframe/Architrave

Wall

Dado Rail/Chair Rail

Door

Dado

Skirting

Floor

EXTERIOR ARCHITECTURAL DETAIL

Ridge Tiles

Roof

Fascia Boards

Window and Frame

Corbel

Front Door and Frame

Plinth

Chimney Stack

Bargeboard

Quoin

FACING PAGE
The use of just one colour —
Eddy — in this bedroom has
created an oasis of calm, in
spite of the panelling and
cupboard being in slightly
conflicting styles. Note that
even the floor is included in
the monochrome scheme, for
the ultimate soothing space.

INSPIRATION

I often think that a Pinterest album is the modern-day equivalent of a scrapbook: a collection of ideas and references to help to inspire, clarify your decisions and shape your approach to decorating your home. It can also be used to make a log of all your decorative choices, to look back at with fondness to the first ideas you had when creating your home.

Start by collecting images of anything with a colour or a combination of colours that you love; these don't have to match, they just need to work together. We are surrounded by colour in our daily lives, from the harmonizing ones in nature to the attention-grabbing colours of advertising billboards. Let your instincts lead you; consider the colours you like to wear, as they are your most obvious form of self-expression.

When I'm thinking about new colours for the Farrow & Ball palette, I like to take pictures of any colours that appeal to me, whether an expansive blue summer sky or a vibrant red child's toy. Do the same for your home; gather together objects of particular beauty, no matter how small or apparently insignificant. Entire decorating schemes can be built around anything from a single cushion to a much loved jug; the iconic colours of Hermès and Tiffany packaging have been the inspiration for many a decorating scheme. If you choose to use existing furniture or curtains in your new scheme, include images or fabric swatches of those in your digital scrapbook too.

FACING PAGE
Inspiration comes in many forms, and decorative schemes evolve from many different sources. A living mood board such as this is a wonderful starting point for deciding which colours you want to live with and which combinations are the most appealing.

THIS PAGE
All the wooden cladding
and trim in photographer
James Merrell's houseboat
are painted in Cornforth
White. The colour provides
the perfect neutral
background for his many
references and inspirations.

can also provide valuable reference, no
e your own home may be. The work of great
Robert Adam, who used striking mixed
as many as six colours on one ceiling, or John
greatest colourist of his generation, can be
ional.

great influence, whether you are drawn to
colours in Mark Rothko's abstract work or
ones of Giorgio Morandi's still lifes. Your wall
hance any work of art you have on display, so
make sure they work well together.

Palettes gathered from your travels are also a rich source of
inspiration, but be wary of using them in your home. The tempting
colours of a dazzling tropical flower may well appear garish out of
bright sunshine.

Whatever your inspiration, it is best to gather as many elements
together as you can, including all floor coverings, tiles and fabrics.
Look at how they react to each other; some colours will recede,
while others will demand your attention, so you may need to
rework the mix. Treat them as ingredients for your own personal
home recipe, each one as delicious and important as the other.
As long as you let your instincts guide you, you will be all set to
embark on your decorating adventure.

RIGHT
The Farrow & Ball colour
fan is an indispensable tool
when choosing colours, as
well as the perfect companion
for checking colours against
flooring or worktops.

3 THINGS
TO THINK ABOUT

There are no hard-and-fast rules when it comes to decorating. Luckily, we all gravitate towards different styles, live in different places and like different colours – the world would be a much duller place if this were not the case. No room is the same, so the choice of colour should be influenced by the particular conditions of the space: how it functions, its architecture and when it is used. However, it is certainly helpful to bear the following three pointers in mind when starting to decorate:

The architectural elements of the room
The light
Your style

FACING PAGE
The fiery qualities of Bamboozle are complemented perfectly by the use of Drop Cloth on the period windows and floor in this sitting room. At night, this east-facing space becomes warm and intimate, but in the morning it feels totally uplifting — the perfect place for a light breakfast.

ARCHITECTURE

Colour can appear to alter the proportions of a room visually, effectively changing its size and shape. Here are some general tips on how to make the most of the architecture you have in your home.

Lighter colours are often best suited to big rooms because they maximize the space and won't feel overpowering. If you have a large room that's full of light, then by using lighter shades you can cherish the light you have. While making a bold statement in a large room can be daunting, because patterns and strong colours can be overwhelming in very large doses, it can also counterbalance the light.

Darker tones will enhance a small room and make it feel more intimate. Think about treating these spaces like a jewellery box, packed with fabulous colour, rather than leaving them drab and monotone.

Strong colours in a small space will disguise the corners so that you can't read the boundaries, and this, in turn, will make the room feel larger. Restricting the number of colours you use will also make it feel bigger.

If you have the unusual conundrum of needing to make your room appear smaller, then a strongly contrasting trim colour, either lighter or darker than the walls, will help to define the space so that it doesn't feel endless.

ABOVE
Painting three walls and the ceiling in All White bestows a certain simplicity on this unusual property, and allows the ancient wooden beams to remain the stars of the show. Meanwhile, the use of rich and warm London Clay on the back wall creates a more intimate and cosy area in this vast space.

FACING PAGE
The owner of this charming town house has been spectacularly adventurous with their choice of colour. Stripes on the walls in the room in the foreground and on the staircase forge the perfect link between the two areas. Green Smoke on the lobby woodwork adds a delightfully informal touch.

Be wary of feature walls, which often cause havoc by playing with a room's proportions. Painting a strong colour on the two longest walls in a room will make them appear closer together, giving the impression of a narrower space. In contrast, a dark wall at one end (or both ends) of a long, thin corridor or room will also have the effect of bringing the walls closer, making the space seem squarer in shape.

Familiarize yourself with all the features in your room; the colours used on each of them are equally important. If your room is an awkward shape, with crushingly low or toweringly high ceilings, these problems can all be solved by the simple use of colour, as outlined in the following chapters.

FACING PAGE
Although charcoal metal
doors and windows have
become increasingly popular,
there is no doubt that wood
painted in one of our darks
has much more character.
Here, Pitch Black has been
used to great effect.

RIGHT
The quirks of the
architecture in this attic
room have been enhanced
by the use of two different
colours on the panelling
— Parma Gray and Wimborne
White — to create the most
charming space.

LIGHT

Light is one of the most important things to take into consideration when choosing colours. If the room you are decorating benefits from bright southern sunshine or indirect northern light (this is for the northern hemisphere and vice versa for the southern), the most important thing is to monitor how its appearance changes throughout the day: in the morning, the light is bluer, at midday it is fairly neutral, while the evening light is somewhat warmer. You will then better understand the effect that light and shade have on colour.

It is always tempting to turn to light colours for small, dark spaces, but this generally results in a dull, visually unappetizing room. Although a strong colour might seem counterintuitive, the results can be wonderfully theatrical and much more exciting than any attempt to create light by painting a room white.

Conversely, large, light rooms are best celebrated with lighter tones, which then lead to glimpses of intriguing darker colours in smaller adjacent rooms.

Interconnecting rooms can benefit from being painted in colours of equal strength to create harmony. However, an entrance hall, especially one with little or no natural light, painted a dark colour exudes glamour at the point of arrival, and every room leading off it feels bigger and brighter.

Now that so many of us are spending more time at home, it makes sense to use lighter colours in the rooms we use during the day and stronger colours to retreat to at night. In this way, we celebrate the natural light and distinguish our working day from our relaxing evenings.

ABOVE
Gorgeous early morning sunshine fills this west-facing space. Very little colour is needed on the walls because the room is all about the natural light. Here, muted blue-grey Hazy (A), is appropriately subtle.

FACING PAGE
The plaster-like softness produced by Setting Plaster on the walls of this sitting room is both rich and relaxed. Filled with natural light during the day, the room becomes a very intimate space at night, when the light from the low pendant lamp makes the walls fall into shadow.

HOW LIGHT IMPACTS COLOUR

Without light there is no colour. The joy of the heavily pigmented Farrow & Ball paints is how their colours change through the course of the day, according to the amount of natural light in a room and the direction that the room faces, as both will have an enormous impact on a colour's appearance. The same paint can look different from room to room, at different times of the day and in different seasons. It's truly magical.

North-facing rooms

Northern light tends to bring out the cooler tones in a colour, so avoid anything with a green or grey base. Yellow-based colours will bounce light around the room, but I think it best not to fight nature. Instead, use stronger colours for dramatic, intimate spaces.

South-facing rooms

South-facing rooms can be full of warm light for most of the day. To maximize this feeling of light and space, use pale tones. Soft blues will create a fresher look while warmer tones will glow.

East-facing rooms

The light in east-facing rooms is wonderfully bright in the morning, becoming more muted in the afternoon and evening. Colours sometimes look a little blue in eastern light, so it is best to work in harmony with cooler, light tones, choosing colours that will retain warmth in the evening but look fresh in the morning.

West-facing rooms

The light in west-facing rooms tends to be more muted in the morning and far more dramatic in the evening. Warm tones will accentuate the light in the afternoon and evening sun, while greyer colours will retain a feeling of light but will change from morning to evening – looking cooler earlier and warmer later.

West- and east-facing rooms

The light changes really dramatically throughout the day in these dual-aspect rooms. Count this as a blessing, as the colours on your walls will constantly surprise and thrill you. It is, however, often best to work out when you spend most of your time in these rooms and tailor your choice of colour to the type of light experienced accordingly.

Artificial light

As with natural light, artificial lighting also affects how colours can appear in a room. Halogen and incandescent bulbs emit a yellow light, making colours appear warmer, while LED bulbs and fluorescent tubes tend to produce a bluer light, giving paint a cooler cast. For the best results, you may want to sample colours with a neutral white bulb, which most accurately replicates daylight.

ABOVE LEFT
The walls and ceiling of this slightly light-deprived bedroom have been painted a timeless Shaded White, while the floor is in slightly paler School House White, to bounce any available light onto the walls. A pure white would have made this room seem dull and stark.

ABOVE RIGHT
Had the ceiling in this north-facing family kitchen been painted a bright white, the room would have felt darker. Instead, warm Stirabout has been used as a counterpoint to the cool natural light.

BELOW

Setting Plaster is always changing according to the different light conditions. In this kitchen, it changes in the most charming way throughout the day, and complements the rather extraordinary shadows.

FACING PAGE

The owners of this impressive kitchen have been very bold in their choice of colour, using Inchyra Blue and Bone, to create a really dramatic space. There's no need to worry about it being dark, as it is filled with natural light during the day and lit by numerous different light sources at night.

LIGHT

STYLE

—

Follow your gut instinct. Choosing a paint colour is as much to do with your lifestyle as it is with the architecture of your home and the light within it. It is vitally important not to use colours simply because they are fashionable; choose those that you really love and feel comfortable with and will stand the test of time. Similarly, be well informed and historically sensitive to your house or apartment, but don't restrict yourself to colours pertinent to the date that it was built. More important is to be yourself. It is your home and no one else should dictate how it looks.

The colours you choose, whether discreet or bold, must work for the way you live your life today. They can be used to define volume, shift focus and give a visual destination but, above all, they should be used to make you feel that you have created a unique space that reflects your personality.

Work out whether you want the paint colour to be the main focus of your decoration or to act purely as a backdrop. The most restful homes tend to have the same palette throughout. This will provide the perfect foundation for whatever style of decor you choose. However, you may prefer to fill your home with beautiful rich shades that reflect you and the way you want to live.

The first impression given by your home should be welcoming. A dramatic colour in the hall will give you licence to make all the rooms leading off it far more neutral, and when painted in a strong colour, it makes every adjoining room feel lighter and bigger. You can also be a little braver in your colour choice because this is a room that is passed through en route to somewhere else.

Dining rooms, which are often lit by candles and chandeliers, also benefit from some drama. Using a stronger colour will throw the walls into shadow and leave the table in the spotlight.

For most families, the kitchen is the hub of the home and it is often best to make it your lightest space. Kitchens are busy places, so the same colour on both the walls and woodwork (excluding units and islands) keeps them simple and serene. This colour can also be used in the rest of the house on all the other woodwork.

Bedrooms are private spaces where we go to relax, so they should be soothing and calming. To infuse a room with a sense of peace, you need to choose colours you are naturally drawn to. Spare rooms, which are used less often, can create much more impact with either a strong colour or a flamboyant wallpaper. The space you create will feel like a gift to your guest.

BELOW LEFT
Painted in Stone Blue, this insignificant window in the basement of a historic house is totally charming and in sync with the style of the rest of the house.

BELOW RIGHT
Although I'm not usually a fan of the feature wall, I adore this room where just the end wall is painted in historic Chine Green (A), to make a backdrop for the kitchen. With the Liberty print curtains, this is a fantastic mix of traditional and industrial styles.

FACING PAGE
There is something delightfully relaxed and familiar about this pared-back kitchen and its mismatched surfaces. The panelling in Shadow White gives the space a homely feel, while the walls are in honest All White.

ABOVE
Great White in our Limewash
finish is perfect for the
walls of this unique space.
It sits comfortably alongside
the historic stone and
weathered wood, painted
in Shaded White, to create
a really appealing room.

FACING PAGE
There is something
irresistible about this
charming kitchen, where
the carefully balanced
combination of Setting
Plaster on both the trim
and cabinets, the slightly
stronger Templeton Pink
on the back wall and School
House White on the other
walls and ceiling create an
exceptionally pleasing space.
This is artful layering!

COLOUR WHEEL

Although very useful for understanding the basic structure of colour, the colour wheel is not always the decorator's best friend, especially when dealing with the subtleties of the Farrow & Ball palette. The infinite combinations and the relationship between colours are oversimplified in the wheel, and there is so much more to creating a successful decorative scheme.

The colour wheel that we are most used to seeing today has 12 sections, made up of primary, secondary and tertiary colours. It can certainly help you to understand how colours relate to each other – those that work together and those that don't.

Colours that sit side by side on the wheel, such as Blue Gray and Mizzle, are known as analogous. Broadly harmonious, together they create natural-looking, tranquil spaces, but be careful to avoid contrasts that are too subtle; they will create a room totally lacking in vitality. Complementary colours are any two that sit directly opposite each other, such as Eating Room Red and Green Smoke. Using complementary colours creates schemes with maximum contrast, resulting in dynamic and exciting rooms.

On the next few pages, using images from houses of varying styles and eras, we explore how the five colour families of Red, Yellow, Green, Blue and Darks affect our homes and our mood.

FACING PAGE
Our interpretation of the colour wheel, using samples of Farrow & Ball colours, was created for the cover of the original version of this book. We couldn't resist including it again here.

RED

———

Adored around the world since the Victorian era, red is a warm and welcoming colour, with a shade to suit every style. It's no wonder it's still a favourite today.

For a slightly formal red, look no further than aged burgundy Eating Room Red, deep crimson Incarnadine or rich Preference Red. Like the slightly cleaner Rectory Red, all these colours have their roots firmly in the past, but they are also perfect for use today, especially on panelling or doors in Full Gloss.

For those who like their reds really spicy, fiery Bamboozle will bring a spirited joy and warmth to any room, as will the equally deep and dramatic, but slightly more playful, Charlotte's Locks. If you're feeling hesitant about these colours, start small; they are particularly suited to very small rooms or the inside of a cupboard.

Who can resist the gentle tones of Pink Ground, Setting Plaster and Templeton Pink? A fabulous blush family in their own right, these colours feel like they are giving you a big hug – and they are especially soothing when used on both walls and ceiling.

Equally relaxing but a little stronger, the wonderfully faded tones of Red Earth and earthy Book Room Red (A) will bring warmth to any scheme, while still feeling gloriously informal – perfect for laid-back living rooms.

Pink offers a beautiful breadth of style. Charming Tailor Tack is our lightest and most delicate pink. Equally pretty are Calamine and Middleton Pink. More lively and vibrant are Nancy's Blushes and attention-grabbing Rangwali, or you could embrace the wildly romantic Cinder Rose. A more muted rose, like moody Sulking Room Pink, or the underlying lilac tones of Peignoir, will create a sophisticated feel.

Our purple tones graduate from fresh Great White and restful Calluna, both favoured in bedrooms, through to the sophisticated lavender tones of Brassica, so often used as an alternative to grey. Meanwhile, deep aubergine Brinjal and the bluer tones of regal Pelt add drama and weight to any space.

FACING PAGE, ABOVE LEFT
I can't think of anything cosier than sitting in front of the fire in this room painted totally in rich Blazer (A). The paint's depth of colour and warmth are outstanding.

FACING PAGE, BELOW LEFT
Although Templeton Pink was originally made for a historic house, it feels just as welcoming in this contemporary hall.

FACING PAGE, ABOVE RIGHT
Fruit Fool (A) is as mouthwatering as its name suggests. The inclusion of some blue pigment in the paint prevents it looking too sugary sweet on this bedroom panelling.

FACING PAGE, BELOW RIGHT
Rectory Red feels clean and modern in this well-lit garden room and is the perfect backdrop for the cascading house plants. Any space painted in this colour will be stimulating.

FACING PAGE
This magnificent dining room has been painted in richly saturated Radicchio (A), which is fiery during the day and warm at night. Joa's White was the perfect choice for the ceiling and cornice, resulting in a low-impact contrast with the walls, to retain a historic feel.

RIGHT
The historic crimson tones of Eating Room Red, combined with deep and dramatic Charlotte's Locks, creates the most beguiling corridor in this colour-packed house.

YELLOW

Yellow, once a mainstay of decoration, had lost favour for a while, but with its nostalgic feel and ability to create a hopeful and optimistic atmosphere, it is once again popular everywhere, from rustic farmhouses to the most contemporary of homes.

Strong and moody India Yellow is the most intense of our yellows. Its unmatched richness can literally make rooms appear to be lit by electric light, while retaining a feel of something from a earlier time.

Bright yellows can also be perceived as sunshine, particularly the uncomplicated tones of refreshing Dayroom Yellow and timeless Yellow Ground, which all create hopeful and optimistic rooms full of energy. Citron, a vibrant lemon yellow, as the name suggests, is also light and refreshing.

These yellows are all fantastically stimulating, bringing rooms to life, which makes them less appropriate for bedrooms, where the soothing tones of Farrow's Cream and Dorset Cream are more suitable. Magical Tallow, with its slight, underlying warmth, creates softer, more reflective spaces.

My favourite yellows, however, are restrained Sudbury Yellow and modest Hay, with their muted sophisticated tones and underlying green. These soft yellows are less intense and sunny than others, producing decorative schemes that feel as if they have been there forever.

PALE HOUND® 71

DAYROOM YELLOW™ 233

YELLOWCAKE® 279

CITRON™ 74

YELLOW GROUND™ 218

BABOUCHE® 223

FACING PAGE
Strong and moody India Yellow is really intense in this bathroom. This deep mustard colour has also been used on the underside of the bathtub, making the room feel bigger.

FACING PAGE, ABOVE LEFT
Clean and vivid Dutch Orange (A) will enliven any room. Its dynamic quality is just perfect to brighten up this dark space and make the bathroom beyond feel lighter.

FACING PAGE, BELOW LEFT
Cane (A) is a very special colour, which, although a strong shade, can feel soft and almost creamy in low light. When artificially lit, it has a surprising brightness and feels suitably modern in this situation.

FACING PAGE, ABOVE RIGHT
The gentle, creamy warmth of traditional Farrow's Cream never fails to produce really inviting rooms that are soft and easy to live with.

FACING PAGE, BELOW RIGHT
How can clean India Yellow fail to make you smile? There couldn't be a more cheerful addition to this kitchen in a delightful shepherd's hut.

ABOVE
Inspired by the lemon trees of California, the soft citrus shade of Citrona (A) cannot fail to impart a sunny feel to a room, even one in the middle of the city. Here, the colour saturates every surface.

GREEN

——

Without doubt, green promotes a sense of well-being and reflects the balanced feeling of nature, which is perhaps why we have welcomed green into our homes with unsurpassed relish recently. Green rooms retain an essence of life unmatched by any other colour and make us feel secure.

Fabulously uncomplicated Beverly and the deep forest green of soothing Studio Green both look greener in bright daylight and more conservative in lower light. Although chosen for contemporary homes, along with rich Calke Green and weathered Green Smoke, they have a traditional flavour that evokes a feeling of calm and serenity.

If you have a taste for the comfortable style of the English country house, then look no further than Lichen and Vert De Terre, which create flexible and restful rooms that are the perfect backdrop to shabby chic furniture and well-loved fabrics.

Equally tranquil and muted, the combination of French Gray with lighter Eddy and darker Treron are really much more green than grey, but characterfully flit between the two, depending on the light and time of day. This new family, all of which can be layered in one space, could not be more relaxed and is perfect for rooms that you would like to connect to the garden.

For a more sophisticated look, Ball Green, an old distemper colour, has a magical quality, appearing almost silver in candlelight, which makes it perfect for dining rooms, as is the darker but equally smoky Card Room Green.

Vital greens like Yeabridge Green are lush and uplifting. Together with cheerful Breakfast Room Green and Whirlybird, it is associated with health and good luck, which creates a happy family atmosphere. Rooms painted in these colours can't fail to bring cheer, and none more so than stimulating but dangerous-sounding Arsenic!

FACING PAGE
This effortless combination of Breakfast Room Green on the walls and Stone Blue on the furniture allows us to revel in a timeless scheme that feels both arresting and familiar.

BELOW LEFT

We added Whirlybird to our palette as an upbeat green that is perfect for a family home. Used on both the walls and the ceiling in this kitchen, it feels fresh and playful and is tempered with a cabinet painted in deeper green Beverly.

BELOW RIGHT

Rich, earthy Olive (A) is the perfect green for rooms deprived of light. In this characterful bedroom, it has been paired with soft pinks in the bed linen — an enduringingly popular combination reminiscent of a spring garden.

BELOW LEFT

The soothing tones of Eddy are the perfect complement to this pared-back kitchen with its varied materials. The bright white skirting and ceiling produce a fresh, uncomplicated look.

BELOW RIGHT

I used Bancha in my hall to echo the hues of the lush garden and create a feeling of security on entering the house. And, of course, it makes the rooms leading off the hall appear much lighter.

BLUE

——

Although blue is the colour used most often in decorating, it certainly tends to divide opinion more than any other. For some, it immediately conjures up cold, unfriendly spaces, while for others it evokes calm and serenity, even cosiness.

Some people are drawn to cooler colours, like classic Parma Gray, which, together with stronger Lulworth Blue, can feel quite formal when contrasted with a bright white, but they are still firm favourites for those who prefer a clean and crisp finish. These two have now been joined by Kittiwake, which has a touch more black pigment, to create a warmer, more relaxed feel, but it is still brighter than silvery Light Blue.

For those who like things light and airy, then illuminating Borrowed Light and the more traditional Skylight are the perfect choice. The aqua qualities of Cabbage White and Pale Powder, with their underlying green, are warmer and prettier. They make up the lightest tones of a colour family that includes Teresa's Green and Green Blue.

A more relaxed family of blues comprises soft Cromarty, modest Mizzle, Blue Gray and stronger Pigeon. These shades work together seamlessly in any combination, and have the almost magical quality of gently shifting between blue and grey, depending on the light and time of day.

Our third family of blues also works as an alternative to grey but feels a lot more modern. Selvedge is a lighter, less grey version of down-to-earth De Nimes, which in turn sits perfectly with aged Inchyra Blue. The lightest member of this family is the similarly aged and ever popular Oval Room Blue.

If you are unafraid of deep blues, then you have a fantastic choice to make between greener Hague Blue, which oozes glamour and is the ultimate in chic; slightly fresher Stiffkey Blue, which manages to feel both dramatic and optimistic; and curiously named Wine Dark, which is just as sophisticated while feeling good for the soul.

FACING PAGE
Nearly everything in this room is blue — which makes a bold statement. The vivid tone of Pea Flower Tea from our Carte Blanche collection on the walls is elevated by the use of Stripe wallpaper in the same colour below the dado rail. The ceiling and trim are in Au Lait which is also the background colour of the paper, so they sit seamlessly together.

BELOW LEFT

Sometimes colours are so popular that we want to offer them in a lighter shade. Selvedge is a lighter version of De Nimes and is ideal in this laid-back kitchen — just the colour for those who like their blues with a big dose of grey.

BELOW CENTRE

I am constantly having to battle with clients who are convinced that rooms painted in blue will always be cold. Here is the proof that it simply isn't true. What could be more vibrant and life-affirming than this delightful sitting room painted in Chinese Blue (A)?

BELOW RIGHT

If you want to create a really upbeat room that stays truly blue in all lights, then Kittiwake is the perfect colour. Painting the cupboard the same colour as the walls means that it does not dominate the space, in spite of its size.

FACING PAGE

It is often best to embrace a dark room, especially if it is used mostly at night. The use of rich Wine Dark in this setting is masterful. Stopping the colour before the ceiling, and painting Kittiwake above, creates a really intimate space with a modern feel.

DARKS

—

MAHOGANY™   36

TANNER'S BROWN®   255

RAILINGS™   31

BLACK BLUE™   95

OFF-BLACK™   57

PITCH BLACK™   256

Many of us have crossed over to the dark side when choosing paint, being less concerned with space and more with mood; deep, saturated colours abound. Contrary to popular opinion, such colours can be an inspired solution in a dark space. They blur boundaries, so you can't read the perimeters of the space, and result in rooms that are a delight to retire to at the end of the day.

At Farrow & Ball, we have more than a dozen of these apparently simple colours, all of which evoke a complex response. The strongest of our greens, Studio Green, reads almost black in low light, as does Paean Black in the red family and classic Railings in the blue. The dark hues in all these colours transform rooms into dramatic and enveloping spaces that have an unexpected hint of modernity, especially when only one colour is used on all the elements in the room.

The latest addition to our selection of darks is Hopper Head, a classic charcoal colour that sits directly between Railings and Down Pipe. All these are undeniably moody and commanding, and are used as much on trim as they are on walls, just like the richer and redder Tanner's Brown.

If your preference is for something a little lighter, then you can choose between the industrial lead tones of Plummett, the moody but less grey Mole's Breath, or Charleston Gray, which, like London Clay, has a warm undertone that gives a certain softness.

All these complex colours have a robust intensity and produce powerful, stimulating rooms, while being respectful of traditional proportions. Together with soft Off-Black, they are more flattering to adjacent colours than an intense jet black.

Of course, we also have wonderful Pitch Black, which is as pure a black as you can get, and is strong and uncomplicated in all lights.

FACING PAGE
The walls in this bedroom are painted in saturated Hopper Head, which has been softened by warm grey Mole's Breath on the door. Importantly, white has been avoided on any woodwork; this would have made the walls look darker and the room feel less relaxed.

FACING PAGE

Few would dare to choose Off-Black for a dining room, let alone take it over onto the ceiling. But in this space, which is used solely at night, it flatters the architecture and creates a mood of refined tranquillity.

ABOVE LEFT

Chine Green (A) is one of our most traditional colours, and it has always been popular for use outside. Here, it works perfectly in a contemporary living room, where it is dramatic but also soft, on account of its earthy nature.

ABOVE RIGHT

Pantalon (A) is a mysterious dark. Neither brown nor green, it is particularly captivating. Here, it makes the perfect backdrop for a very special collection of porcelain. Using two colours on the shelves creates an extra stylish edge.

NEUTRALS

Neutrals will always play a part in decorating because there are so many people who feel most comfortable when surrounded by carefully balanced colours that create an understated environment and make few demands on the eye. They offer infinite possibilities for making spaces airy and relaxing, refined and timeless, or elegantly sophisticated.

However, neutrals alone are not a fail-safe combination and it is all too easy to fall into the trap of using bland, depressing colours that are nothing like the subtle, complex palettes featured here.

Farrow & Ball has six established neutral groups. Our Relaxed Neutrals, Architectural Neutrals and Contemporary Neutrals all have a greyer bias, while our Timeless Neutrals, Warm Neutrals and Traditional Neutrals are a little softer in feel.

Although each group will produce a very different look, the four shades within each one can be relied upon to work perfectly together in seemingly endless permutations, to create an effortless flow and variety of moods in your home.

FACING PAGE
There is a very appealing air of simplicity about the hall in this country house. Every surface has been painted in All White, which is exactly what it says: a totally pure white without the colder blue undertones of a brilliant white. Here, it feels soft and sympathetic to the beautiful parquet floor.

TRADITIONAL NEUTRALS

This inimitable group of neutrals has its roots firmly in the past – they were the original signature 'whites' shown by Lime White being colour No.1. Traditional in feel, their colours are sophisticated and restrained in equal measure.

The underlying grey-green tones of this complex palette have a softness that results in decorative schemes that feel as if they have been in place forever.

One of the most effective ways of using Traditional Neutrals to create a special atmosphere is by layering one upon another in a room, for example, mid-colour Off-White on the walls, darker Old White on woodwork, Lime White on any moulding or coving, and Slipper Satin on the ceiling.

This group works perfectly with muted colours, and prevents woodwork and ceilings feeling too clean and bright.

TIMELESS NEUTRALS

Of all the neutral groups, Timeless Neutrals have the widest appeal, sitting between the slightly more yellow Traditional Neutrals and the greyer Relaxed Neutrals. Neither too warm nor too cool, this special group is often seen as a 'safe pair of hands'.

These perfectly balanced stony colours reflect the soft tones of white in increasingly deep shade. The difference between them is deliberately subtle and can be lost in the dark areas of a room, but there is always a combination within these four tones that will work to enhance your home.

An easy scheme that will suit architecture of any type or date is to paint Drop Cloth, the darkest tone in the group, on panelling and Shadow White or Shaded White on the walls, complemented by a ceiling in School House White.

WARM NEUTRALS

Neutrals are at their best when used with others of a similar tone, and the unassuming colours of the Warm Neutrals sit perfectly together. Their red base results in the warmest schemes of all the neutrals. Together, they create ageless and understated colour schemes, making a room feel especially welcoming. Use them on ceilings and trim with any red tones to soften the contrast between walls and woodwork.

Warm Neutrals are a perfect match for exteriors too. The strongest colour in the group, Oxford Stone, is reminiscent of Cotswold stone and a natural choice for masonry, while the slightly lighter Joa's White works particularly well alongside, on quoins and fascia boards. Dimity could then be used on window frames, with delicate Pointing on glazing bars, to create the most seamless and undemanding of schemes.

'Dimity'

'Pointing'

'Oxford Stone'

'Joa's White'

FACING PAGE

There is something so comforting about this room painted in our warmest neutrals — it simply glows, even on the dullest of days. Joa's White on the walls sits seamlessly with Dimity on the ceiling and London Stone on the units. The Calke Green island injects a little extra energy into the space.

CONTEMPORARY NEUTRALS

This group of greys brings an edge to decorative schemes while imparting a certain warmth. Their magic lies in an underlying lilac tone, which makes them perfect for those who want to avoid anything too cool or sombre.

The four enriching shades flatter each other and have a refined sophistication while remaining understated. As a group, they are often used throughout an entire home, so you can drift from room to room hardly noticing that there has been a change of shade. Use the strongest tone, Dove Tale, in the hall, to create a sense of drama; Elephant's Breath for relaxed living areas; and Strong White in the kitchen, where it feels a natural choice alongside stainless-steel fittings and will make the kitchen the airiest room in the home. The woodwork throughout could then be painted in versatile Skimming Stone.

FACING PAGE
Despite the fact that this set of neutrals was originally conceived for contemporary homes, the extraordinary warmth in their underlying lilac tone makes them a natural choice for all sorts of styles. Here, the walls have been painted in classic Elephant's Breath, with sympathetic Skimming Stone on the frieze and ceiling. Had a brighter white been used here, the room would have lost its effortless feel.

'Elephant's Breath'

'Dove Tale'

'Strong White'

'Skimming Stone'

RELAXED NEUTRALS

The Relaxed Neutrals group creates a look that is ultimately easy to live with and will suit almost any style of architecture. Ideal for those who prefer understated decoration, these completely harmonious colours are enormously versatile. The four shades are natural and quiet, with a quality that is hard to pin down, but they will always result in the perfect environment for relaxation.

With little bias to either warmer or cooler tones, this group can be used in any combination together and with most other colours: Purbeck Stone on the walls, with Cornforth White woodwork and Wevet or Ammonite on the ceiling, will create the subtlest of looks, almost as if you have used only one colour and the differences in tone are shadows. The minimal aesthetic of this combination will promote simple, calm and easy modern living.

ARCHITECTURAL NEUTRALS

This is the perfect group of neutrals for those wanting a stronger architectural or modern industrial feel, or indeed for those prefering a 'pure' grey. Purposely cool, with a bluer undertone than the other neutrals, these colours have a look that is conducive to minimal living

These four shades are particularly impactful when combined with stronger tones, so work beautifully in the modern home.

Blackened, the lightest tone of the Architectural Neutrals, often features on both walls and ceilings throughout the home, to create a light and seamless space. The strongest tone, Pavilion Gray, on the floor will ground the scheme, while Dimpse and Blackened used in small rooms or as accents on furniture will add interest. Clean All White on the ceilings and trim will create simple, uncluttered spaces.

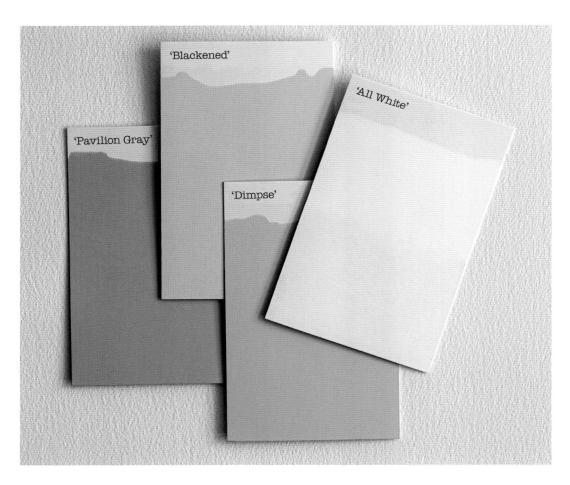

FACING PAGE
Although this Brooklyn hall has an air of simplicity about it, the colours on the walls and trim work deceptively well together. Cool, grey Dimpse is used on the panelling and walls, while the doors are painted in its lighter counterpart, Blackened. These Architectural Neutrals sit perfectly with the grey oak floor, to make a modern, clean-feeling space.

NEUTRAL ACCENTS

Even if you choose to live with a really understated colour scheme, such as those outlined over the last few pages, a stronger accent colour of a similar tone can shift the balance of the room, for added interest and impact. By including a deeper colour within the scheme, you will make the other colours in the neutral family come alive. The best accent colours for each family are as follows:

- Traditional Neutrals: Mouse's Back
- Timeless Neutrals: Pigeon
- Warm Neutrals: London Stone
- Contemporary Neutrals: Charleston Gray
- Relaxed Neutrals: Mole's Breath
- Architectural Neutrals: Down Pipe

These accent colours can be incorporated in a number of different ways, from painting entire walls to small pieces of furniture, introducing an extra element to the decoration.

SAMPLING

———

How a colour behaves in relation to other colours and in different light conditions is extremely complex, and nothing beats seeing them all in situ. Your perception of the colour will almost certainly change when you look at it in different light conditions and as the day progresses. Although our colour cards are created with real paint (no printing for Farrow & Ball), there really is no substitute for testing proposed colours in the room where they will be used. Here are some pointers:

- Don't paint sample colours directly onto the wall – it's very distracting and they are difficult to remove.
- Paint two coats of your sample pot colour onto a couple of pieces of paper or card – the larger, the better – and place them in two different areas of the room.
- Check them at different times throughout the day and see how the colour changes – you'll be amazed.
- If you are decorating a space used exclusively at night, look at the colours with the curtains closed; you might even light a candle.
- Sightlines are crucial for creating the right flow through your house, so note how a colour sits with others in adjoining spaces.
- If sampling several colours, do each one in isolation. A patchwork on the wall is really difficult to read, as you are always comparing one colour to another.
- It's very important to look at your wall colour alongside your trim colour in the right proportions; this will affect the way you perceive both tones.

RIGHT
You may wonder why, when I constantly advise against painting samples directly onto the wall, this image is included here. But who can resist a neutral colour card brought to life in this magnificent panelled hall? Each sample is surrounded by the white of the panelling, making the colours easier to read individually.

PART TWO

—

THE
MANUAL

FACING PAGE
With the most serene scheme
of Light Blue on the walls,
and Setting Plaster on the
floor and woodwork, this
room feels blissfully
calm. It is all set off
by an upcycled sideboard
painted in Skimming Stone.

95

WHICH WHITE?

———

Even after making the painstaking decision as to which colour to use on the walls, many of us are equally blinded by the range of whites for ceilings and trim. The following is a handy reference of the complementary white to use with each Farrow & Ball colour. These selected whites match the undertones of the colour they're paired with, to create a look that's refined and expansive. They're designed to make life easier and are also referenced on our colour card, and the complementary whites for our entire range, including our Archive, can be found on our website. You can use them in total confidence.

A

All White / Strong White
Ammonite / Wevet
Arsenic / Wevet

B

Babouche / New White
Ball Green / Slipper Satin
Bamboozle / Slipper Satin
Bancha / Shaded White
Beverly / Shaded White
Blackened / All White
Blue Gray / School House White
Blue Ground / Wevet
Bone / Wimborne White
Borrowed Light / Wevet
Brassica / Great White
Breakfast Room Green / Slipper Satin
Brinjal / Skimming Stone

C

Cabbage White / Wevet
Calamine / All White
Calke Green / Slipper Satin
Calluna / Great White
Card Room Green / Shaded White

Charleston Gray / Strong White
Charlotte's Locks / Strong White
Cinder Rose / Strong White
Citron / Pointing
Cooking Apple Green / Wimborne White
Cook's Blue / Slipper Satin
Cord / White Tie
Cornforth White / Wevet
Cromarty / School House White

D

Dayroom Yellow / Wimborne White
Dead Salmon / Dimity
De Nimes / Shaded White
Dimity / Pointing
Dimpse / Blackened
Dix Blue / Wevet
Dorset Cream / White Tie
Dove Tale / Strong White
Down Pipe / Blackened
Drop Cloth / School House White

E

Eating Room Red / Dimity
Eddy / School House White
Elephant's Breath / Strong White —

F

Farrow's Cream / White Tie
French Gray / Slipper Satin

G

Great White / All White
Green Blue / Wevet
Green Ground / Pointing
Green Smoke / Shaded White

H

Hague Blue / Wevet
Hardwick White / School House White
Hay / Wimborne White
Hopper Head / Blackened

I

Incarnadine / Dimity
Inchyra Blue / Drop Cloth
India Yellow / New White

J

James White / All White
Jitney / Dimity
Joa's White / Dimity

K

Kittiwake / Strong White

L

Lamp Room Gray / Blackened
Lichen / Slipper Satin
Light Blue / School House White
Light Gray / Slipper Satin
Lime White / Slipper Satin
London Clay / Strong White
London Stone / Dimity
Lulworth Blue / Blackened

M

Manor House Gray / Pavilion Gray
Matchstick / White Tie
Middleton Pink / All White
Mizzle / School House White
Mole's Breath / Ammonite
Mouse's Back / Slipper Satin

N

Nancy's Blushes / All White
New White / White Tie

O

Off-Black / Blackened
Off-White / Slipper Satin
Old White / Slipper Satin
Oval Room Blue / Ammonite
Oxford Stone / Dimity

P

Paean Black / Skimming Stone
Pale Powder / Wimborne White
Parma Gray / Blackened
Pavilion Gray / Blackened
Peignoir / Strong White
Pelt / Skimming Stone
Picture Gallery Red / Dimity
Pigeon / School House White
Pink Ground / Wimborne White
Pitch Black / Dimpse
Plummett / Blackened
Pointing / All White
Preference Red / Joa's White
Purbeck Stone / Wevet

R

Railings / Blackened
Rangwali / Great White
Rectory Red / Strong White
Red Earth / Dimity

S

School House White / Wimborne White
Selvedge / Shadow White
Setting Plaster / School House White
Shaded White / School House White
Shadow White / School House White
Skimming Stone / Strong White
Skylight / Wevet
Slipper Satin / Wimborne White
Stiffkey Blue / Ammonite

Stirabout / Pointing
Stone Blue / Ammonite
Stony Ground / School House White
String / White Tie
Strong White / All White
Studio Green / Off-White
Sudbury Yellow / White Tie
Sulking Room Pink / Skimming Stone

T

Tallow / Wimborne White
Tailor Tack / Wimborne White
Tanner's Brown / Joa's White
Templeton Pink / Stirabout
Teresa's Green / School House White
Treron / Off-White

V

Vardo / Ammonite
Vert De Terre / Pointing

W

Wevet / Cornforth White
Whirlybird / James White
White Tie / Wimborne White
Wimborne White / All White
Wine Dark / Ammonite
Worsted / Ammonite

Y

Yeabridge Green / Ammonite
Yellow Ground / White Tie

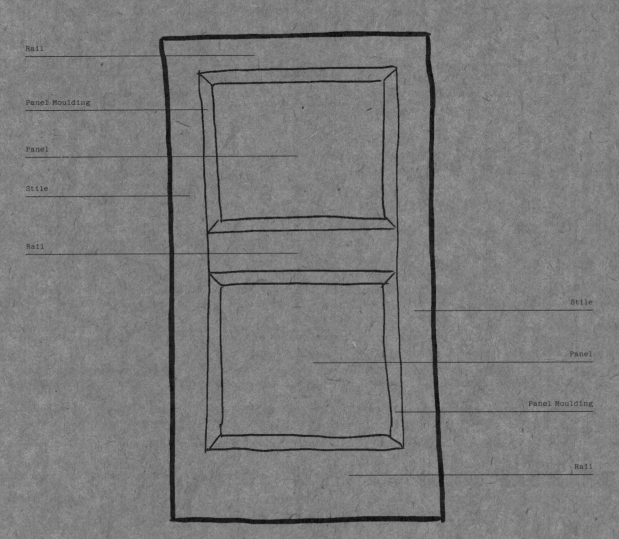

Rail

Panel Moulding

Panel

Stile

Rail

Stile

Panel

Panel Moulding

Rail

WHAT GOES WHERE

Darkest colour: Stiles and rails.

Mid-colour: Panels.

Lightest colour: Panel mouldings.

FACING PAGE

On the walls, Light Sand (A), sits peacefully with London Stone on the panelling — a pairing of two colours inspired by both sides of the Atlantic.

WAYS OF
DECORATING

There are many different ways to decorate a room, and how you choose to approach it is an opportunity to express your own personal style.

When faced with a room made up of seemingly complicated architectural elements, choosing where each colour should go can be a little overwhelming. However, there are only three basic ways to decorate. These are:

White trim with coloured walls
This is the traditional method, and many people feel most comfortable with it.

Trim that is darker than the walls
Much favoured for its relaxed appeal and for making a space appear lighter.

Using the same colour on both walls and trim
This makes a space feel bigger and less fussy.

WHITE TRIM AND COLOURED WALLS

The most traditional way to decorate a room is to use a colour on the walls and a white on the woodwork.

Having the same 'white' on all the woodwork (and the ceiling) is an easy way to unify and connect all the rooms in your home. A bright white, however, can destroy a room where there are muted, subtle colours on the walls, and this is where the Farrow & Ball whites are second to none. For every colour, there is a complementary white, to create a softer, airier atmosphere. If the contrast between your walls and woodwork is strong, your eye will be drawn to where the two colours meet, defining the space and making you more aware of each architectural element, so the room feels smaller. If these features are all softened by a white that sits tonally with the colour of the wall, you will notice them less and the room will feel bigger and calmer. These tone-on-tone schemes create quieter, more seamless rooms. Don't be afraid to use a different complementary white in each room – they will still balance in overall flow.

Rooms painted in stronger more positive tones can benefit from a brighter white, such as All White, which makes a home look fresh and uncomplicated. Using white gloss was almost standard for many years, before its perceived austerity made it fall out of favour. Things have come full circle, though, and it is popular once more, loved for its freshness, crisp contrast and simplicity.

ABOVE
The rich deep teal tones of Coppice Blue (A) will introduce a little drama into any interior. Seen here, contrasted with Clunch (A) on the woodwork, it positively sings.

FACING PAGE
Restored cupboards that have stood the test of time somehow command to be painted in simple white tones to retain some authenticity. Here the soft white Au Lait sits perfectly against spicy brown Cardamon. This combination shows both colours to their best.

BELOW LEFT

This dining area is the epitome of calm and restraint with its Pink Drab (A) walls and Wevet trim. This may look simple but these two colours are the perfect pairing, as both have a hint of underlying grey.

BELOW RIGHT

The strength of colour on the Stiffkey Blue walls makes the woodwork and ceiling look almost white, even though they have been painted in Shaded White, a subtle grey, chosen because it sits comfortably with the stone of the fire surround.

BELOW LEFT
The trim and ceilings of this stylish home in Copenhagen are painted in All White, creating a continuous flow throughout the house. This pure white is the perfect counterpoint to the numerous strong colours on the walls. Here, you see Down Pipe and India Yellow.

BELOW RIGHT
The extraordinary light in this space has been enhanced by the use of School House White on most of the surfaces, but it is the introduction of Card Room Green that builds a fantastic relationship with the garden beyond, framed perfectly by the lighter-coloured window.

DARK TRIM WITH LIGHTER WALLS

The second method of decorating is to make all the trim darker than the walls.

Most people want to create as much light and space in a room as they can, and using a lighter colour on the walls, which is the biggest space, with a darker tone on the woodwork, is the easiest way to achieve this. The dark trim instantly makes the walls feel lighter and introduces a decorative element to your scheme. While this may feel like an intimidating prospect, remember how easily we accept rooms in which the woodwork is unpainted, and we are able to appreciate a rich mahogany or a plain pine. That thought just has to be transferred into paint colour.

The use of a very slightly darker colour on the woodwork provides simple decoration while maintaining a degree of calm, and the Farrow & Ball neutral groups that sit together so seamlessly are perfect for this.

Painting a strong colour on the woodwork and a pale colour on the walls has seen a great resurgence in popularity recently. The look is ideal if you want to make a bold statement on a small scale. As the dark architectural elements draw the eye, changing both the room's focal point and its sense of scale, you should be careful not to let them become overwhelming.

FACING PAGE
This daring combination of wonderfully versatile Castle Gray (A) on the walls, with the slightly deeper but equally smouldering Green Smoke on the woodwork, is utterly inspired and brings huge interest to this otherwise featureless space.

ABOVE RIGHT
This Parisian home is full of natural light, so the owner has wisely chosen to keep the walls light in colour, painting them in understated Slipper Satin. However, Off-Black Full Gloss adds a big dose of glamour and unifies this door with all the others in the apartment.

ABOVE LEFT

The addition of Pigeon
on the stairs in this
delightful cottage has added
tremendously to its overall
charm. Note how the colour
has been used on all the
elements of the staircase,
including the underside, and
works perfectly in making the
School House White walls feel
even lighter than they are.

ABOVE RIGHT

Using the lightest colour
on the largest surface
makes this room feel big
and bright. Strong White
on the walls contrasts with
the darker Lamp Room Gray
on the woodwork, making
the colour selection look
properly considered,
while keeping the space
neutral in tone.

ABOVE LEFT
The light grey undertone of Strong White often gives a slightly urban feel, but here it sits perfectly in a country boot room. It feels utterly timeless contrasted with classic Down Pipe on the doorframe, while the door itself remains white — an effortless combination.

ABOVE RIGHT
The unique depth of grey-pink Peignoir is set off to perfection with the use of Tar (A) on the door, but not its frame. Both these colours are soft and restrained. Combining them results in the most romantic of schemes.

ONE COLOUR

The third method of decorating is to use one colour on both the walls and the woodwork.

There is great historic precedent for this form of decorating. It is also a firm favourite with contemporary decorators because rooms painted in this way are both tranquil and impactful.

Over the years we have taken to highlighting trim, such as picture and chair rails, skirting and architraves, but these are essentially functional rather than decorative elements in our rooms. Don't be afraid to make them 'disappear' by painting them the same colour as the walls.

When a single colour is used, a room suddenly feels bigger – having no contrast means that you are less aware of the confines of the space.

Many people are scared of using dark colours on woodwork, particularly windows, but it is amazing how natural it feels, even if the colour is strong. Ugly, small or plain trim disappears into the wall colour and you really only notice the shadow that it casts.

Another bonus of using one colour is that it connects the interior with the exterior, blending the garden and room together. If your window woodwork is the same colour as the walls, the eye does not stop to register a second colour and glides straight out to the view.

FACING PAGE

The formulation of our Dead Flat finish, once the domain of specialist decorators, has been brought right into the modern world. It still has its extraordinarily matt finish but with added toughness, so it can be used on every surface — perfect for colour-drenching a room such as this charming nursery painted in Setting Plaster.

RIGHT

Many people opt for All White on every single surface in their home. Far from showing a lack of imagination, this conscious decision promotes a calm but strong, stress-free look.

ABOVE LEFT

Many of us are now searching
for space at home in which to
work, and this area painted
in a single colour provides
the perfect 'no distraction'
solution. Broccoli Brown (A),
a quiet, dark stone colour,
sits effortlessly with the
wooden desk, its muted
quality making it ideal
for helping concentration.

ABOVE RIGHT

The use of a single colour,
De Nimes, in this room is
inspired. Not only does
it help to unite the large
amount of joinery and
woodwork, but also creates
a really strong, confident-
looking space. Had the
woodwork been picked out in
a white, the room would have
been broken up into small,
unsatisfactory elements.

ABOVE LEFT

The view from this garden room is more than spectacular, so Green Smoke has been used on every surface, not only to create a connection with the exterior, but also to prevent there being any barrier between the room and the valley beyond.

ABOVE RIGHT

There is nothing calmer than a room painted in just one colour. Here, Berrington Blue (A) is taken from the bottom of the skirting, over the walls and picture rail, up to the ceiling. Even the fire surround is painted in the same colour, creating a space that is totally undemanding but very stylish.

OVERLEAF

Colour-drenching has taken the decorative world by storm, and what could be more beautiful than this room where every surface is painted in beautiful Beverly — a fitting tribute to the colleague it was named after — in our Dead Flat finish.

THIS PAGE
The beauty of this mural
is indisputable, but what
makes it doubly fantastic
in this hall is that many
of the colours in the rooms
leading off it are taken
from the design, creating a
subconscious and very artful
flow through the house. The
background is painted in
delicate Tailor Tack, while
the trees have been created
using different sample pots.

FLOW

Many people want to create a flow through their home, seeing it as paramount in producing an unchallenging environment where you can drift seamlessly from room to room without being jolted by the use of colour. This, of course, can easily be achieved with just one colour. White, which for some represents restraint and purity, is cold, bland and sterile to others. Certainly, walls recede when painted white and reflect light, which makes a room feel bigger. However, this does not necessarily create a relaxed atmosphere.

Using the carefully balanced shades of white and off-white, as outlined in the Neutrals section of this book (see pages 76–91), will prevent rooms from feeling lifeless while retaining a sense of continuity. Each neutral family, with its own personality and characteristics, can be used in any combination to create a flow throughout the home. The possible combinations of the four colours are virtually endless, and you should feel confident in using them for a calm and cohesive look.

Using the same colour for every ceiling in your home is a simple but effective way to create flow. Although you may not even be aware that all the ceilings are painted the same tone, the subconscious effect is both calming and comforting. This does not, however, mean that you should default to a bland and characterless white. Look at the lightest colour you have chosen for the walls in your home and use it on all the ceilings.

SIGHTLINES

Colour can shift our focus and give us a visual destination, so it is often useful to work with colours that are connected tonally in order to create a sense of flow.

If you start with the strongest tone of a colour family, such as Treron, in a hallway, then use the slightly lighter French Gray in the room beyond, and the even lighter Eddy in the room furthest away, this lightest room helps to achieve a greater sense of space and a pleasing pull through the house.

ABOVE LEFT AND RIGHT
These two interconnecting rooms are prettiness personified. The undoubted flow between the two is achieved by taking the wall colour in one and using it to complement the furniture of the other. Berrington Blue (A) and Potted Shrimp (A) sit happily together, united by Wimborne White on the trim and floor.

FACING PAGE
Considering the sightlines from the hall to other rooms is imperative. This combination just makes my heart sing! The vintage feel of Dix Blue in the hall is the perfect complement to the slightly softer Saxon Green (A) in the living room. The two rooms are united by Strong White on the trim and ceiling, which gives the overall scheme a fresh look.

ONE WOODWORK COLOUR

Using a single colour for all the woodwork is the easiest way to create a cohesive look in the home. In fact, it is often useful to have the same colour on both the ceilings and woodwork, to give a fresh and uncomplicated scheme. If you have a room with mouldings framing the doorways leading to other rooms, then using one colour on the trim forms a pleasing link that will create a visual bridge between each space.

ABOVE AND FACING PAGE
The rich deep tone of Monkey Puzzle (A) has been used on all the woodwork in this country cottage, tying all the spaces together and making the bedrooms in Light Blue and Smoked Trout (A) look even more charming. It has also been used for an accent wall below the stairs, along with the radiator, to create a cosy reading nook.

ONE ACCENT COLOUR

There is, of course, always the option of choosing one accent colour and using it in different ways in every room. This works especially well if you also have the same accent colour on, say, the staircase in your hall, the inside of a living room bookcase and a kitchen island. There are a million ways to introduce an accent colour into a room and, by dint of this, create a ribbon of colour throughout your home. To explore the possibilities further, look at Transform Space With Colour on page 127.

ABOVE
The deeply coloured walls
of these linked rooms in
beguiling India Yellow and
intense Green Smoke are a
surprising combination that
works to perfection. Despite
being from totally different
colour families, the similar
depths of colour mean that
they work flawlessly together.
The yellow room is filled with
sun during the day while the
green room is more intimate
and used mostly at night.

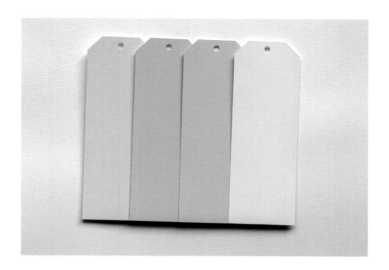

SEVERAL COLOURS

If you wish to unite different parts of the house with a cohesive look but still want to use a range of colours, then it is best to consider your colour choices floor by floor. In this way, you can envision how the colours in adjacent rooms will complement one another. If you stand in your hall, you can see into several rooms. If the relationship between these rooms is not taken into consideration, there will be no overall harmony.

Different colours used in various rooms on the same floor should all have the same tonal weight. For example, sumptuous Wine Dark in one room will sit harmoniously alongside the equally rich Green Smoke and Bamboozle, but it may feel too heavy against fresh Green Ground and delicate Middleton Pink. To work in harmony with these shades, you would need to pick a much lighter, cleaner blue, such as Skylight, in order to create an equally weighted floor of rooms.

In recent times, though, the flow of colours through a house has been deemed much less important than it used to be. Our new found love of stronger tones across different rooms means that the overall atmosphere of our homes has become more important than a seamless flow.

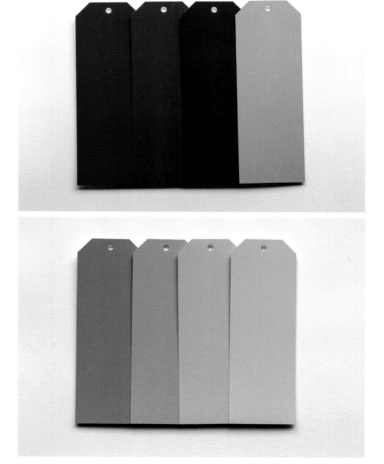

A UNIFYING HALL COLOUR

Halls can unify because they are usually visible from every room on the same floor, so the colour of your hall is definitely the most important when it comes to maintaining a sense of flow. It is advisable to choose it before any of the other room colours.

A hall's decorative scheme serves two purposes: to create an impression on arrival, which sets the tone for the whole house, and, more importantly, to unite different parts of the house, so that there is a smooth visual transition between rooms that might be decorated in a variety of styles and colours. Don't be alarmed by the idea of using a strong colour in the hall – remember, you are always just going to pass through it on the way to somewhere else.

Using a darker tone in the hall, such as Inchyra Blue or Bancha, will not only spark interest and excitement on arrival, but will also make every room leading off it feel bigger and lighter.

FACING PAGE, ABOVE LEFT
This elegant hall painted in classic Cornforth White, with Wimborne White trim, is the ultimate in understated elegance and the perfect foil for all the colour-filled rooms leading off it.

FACING PAGE, ABOVE RIGHT
The clean, cool tones of Kittiwake on every surface in this hall are really thrilling. Such a strong central colour also gives you licence to be much more neutral in other rooms.

FACING PAGE, BELOW LEFT
The entrance to this homely cottage is through the kitchen painted in charming Pink Ground. An inspired colour choice, it creates the most welcoming impression and sets the tone for the rest of the property.

RIGHT
The relationship between Setting Plaster in the hall and Light Blue in the bedroom feels seamless because both paints have the same depth of colour. However, the link between the rooms is secured by using the hall colour on the trim and floor in the bedroom — subtle but incredibly effective.

TRANSFORM SPACE
WITH COLOUR

Colour is not only a visual pleasure but also a powerful tool for transforming spaces. The way we use it to enhance our homes has drastically changed over the last decade, with the small accent giving way to the bolder statement. Colour is now being used in amazingly imaginative ways.

Forget the concept of painting between the skirting/base board and the coving/moulding – or even being constricted by trim. All the rules have been torn up, much to my glee. Over the next few pages, you will see that the smallest amounts of colour used in unusual ways can transform a space from ordinary to extraordinary. And areas can be zoned by colour to bring unexpected delight as well as to define their use. But however brave you may feel, don't forget that an accent colour should enhance rather than overwhelm the rest of your decorative scheme.

FACING PAGE
Each new colour we develop for the Farrow & Ball palette is created for its own individual merits, but sometimes it is fun to look at them as a whole. Here, 11 colours were used to create this fabulous patchwork — an interior for the bold, as well as the dog!

ABOVE LEFT
This unusual landscape window has been made to look bigger by the surrounding band of Pantalon (A) on the wall painted in Berrington Blue (A). The effect is made all the more pleasing by the addition of the low-lying sofa, which echoes the shape of the window.

LEFT
A great example of where more is more, and of how Farrow & Ball colours, be they bright or subtle, work seamlessly together. Embrace fantastically vivid Blue Maize on the walls in Dead Flat and team with Lobster cabinets in the same finish. Then add a twist of Hog Plum on the legs for a cohesive scheme, which can't help but make you smile.

ABOVE RIGHT
This hugely imaginative scheme takes Sugar Bag Light (A) on the wall and replicates it in a stripe that runs across the floor and up the wall, which has been painted in chalky white Clunch (A). Note how, in order to prevent the end of the room feeling cut off, the stripe does not hit the ceiling.

FACING PAGE
Our love affair with having green in our homes is far from over. All green tones feel grounding and connect us with the natural world. And if you love a colour, then why not use it on every surface, as in this super-stylish room painted totally in Calke Green?

FACING PAGE, ABOVE LEFT
The red undertone of Cola (A) sits perfectly against the less intense, earthy yellow Cane (A) in an unorthodox but powerful scheme that both challenges and delights.

FACING PAGE, ABOVE RIGHT
Adding the rich burgundy tones of Eating Room Red to the interior of these much loved kitchen shelves painted in Green Smoke turns them from ordinary into something rather special.

FACING PAGE, BELOW LEFT
Using sophisticated Brinjal in Modern Eggshell on these shelves for boots is totally indulgent. It can't fail to bring joy as well as the toughest of durable finishes.

FACING PAGE, BELOW RIGHT
A visit to the larder in this house is certainly an adventure. Rich Rangwali on the walls and shelves is the perfect partner for sumptuous Pelt on the woodwork.

LEFT
The hours could easily fly by cocooned in this utterly delicious bed nook, The warmth of Oxford Stone on all the surfaces is embellished by a colour pop of Copenhagen Roof (A) on the alcove interior, to create an irresistible private den.

SMALL SURPRISES

For those who prefer an understated environment, colour or pattern can be introduced in tiny amounts in places that may well be hidden for 90 per cent of the time.

The interiors of kitchen units or closets, pocket doors or the underside of a bathtub painted in uplifting colours will achieve an element of surprise without affecting the overall mood and style of a room.

BELOW
Painted in lively Drawing Room
Blue (A), this outsized bookshelf
is essentially a feature wall
that greets you upon entering
the room. The clean, graphic feel
of the colour is counterbalanced
by the soft, subtle tones of
Light Gray on the other walls.

FACING PAGE
This audacious feature wall
is certainly the star of the
room. Painted in a graphic
checkerboard of Wimborne
White and Pantalon (A), it
feels clean and modern, while
retaining a certain warmth.
Creating a pattern like this

is much easier than you might
think, as long as you have
plenty of masking tape and
an equal amount of nerve.

FEATURE WALLS

Colour drastically adjusts our sense of space, and while large, awkwardly shaped rooms can be helped by painting a single wall in a different colour as a focal point, a feature wall can just as easily change the proportions of a room, so think carefully about which wall you choose for this treatment.

A bold colour on one long wall with a lighter colour on the other three, will make the short walls look as if they are being squeezed together, so that the room appears longer and thinner. Colour on one long wall in a bedroom will also create an uncomfortable room to sleep in because of the resulting uneven nature of the space. A feature wall in a bedroom should be behind the bedhead, to ground the room and promote a calm atmosphere.

The use of a stronger colour on a short wall can make a room feel squarer in shape. For example, a long, thin room painted in Wevet, with a bolder tone like Charlotte's Locks on a short wall, will foreshorten the space, helping to make it appear more evenly proportioned.

TRANSFORM SPACE WITH COLOUR

ABOVE

This dresser must change colour more often than any other in the world. At this point, it was painted in rich red-brown Cola (A), joining other friends from our Archive Collection — Sloe Blue (A) on the table legs and Olive (A) on the chairs — to create a colourful but relaxed atmosphere, much enhanced by the very special floral-patterned pink velvet on the inside of the dresser.

FACING PAGE, LEFT

The owner of this bedroom has wisely created a feature wall behind the bed, which serves to ground the room. This delightful Gable wallpaper (BP 5404) in Hague Blue and Green Blue is utterly charming. Depicting traditional village and farmyard scenes with clean, modern styling, its large-scale statement pattern is studded with little details that spark the imagination, taking on added character as you look.

FACING PAGE, RIGHT

Paean Black and Preference Red may be colours that were inspired by artefacts from the past — the leather of vintage bibles and baroque fabrics found in Venetian villas — but here they work beautifully together to create a sumptuous but contemporary scheme.

CREATING EXTRA IMPACT

Make doors and windows appear bigger by extending the paint colour on the frame onto the walls and ceiling. Similarly, give pictures and mirrors extra impact by painting wide borders around them on the wall.

If your window or skylight sits in a recess, then consider painting the reveals in a feature colour. Lively yellows, such as Babouche and Citron, are particularly effective at making a room feel constantly sunny.

Painting a door and its frame in an exuberant colour, such as fiery red Bamboozle, and particularly in Full Gloss for a touch of glamour, gives an extra decorative twist. Although this technique has its roots in the past, it sits extremely well in the modern home.

Striking wallpaper, as well as paint, can also be used to create additional impact. Cover a plain bedhead or delineate a zoned workspace with wallpaper, or line the back of shelves or a dresser with it. Nothing adds more glamour to a cupboard than an unexpected colour or pattern on the inside.

LEFT

I am always looking for ways to introduce more colour into a space. Here, the obvious opportunity to add colour to the divide between the rooms was too good to miss. The addition of even this very small amount of spicy Bamboozle totally changes the atmosphere in this house.

BELOW LEFT

A late addition to this room was a dose of Bamboozle on the interior of the skylight, which has changed the spirit of this room painted in delicate Tailor Tack. The flame-red tones reflect a warm light into the room and are a delightful surprise when you look upwards.

BELOW RIGHT

The young family living in this unique house may have treated the Pavilion Blue (A) walls and elaborate Wimborne White plasterwork in a traditional way, but their mischievous sense of play got the better of them when they introduced the bands of vibrant Cook's Blue on the pillar to make this hall completely their own.

THIS PAGE
The use of three colours in
this space has been executed
with immense skill, both
practically and aesthetically
— strong Hague Blue on the
lower walls, historic Oval
Room Blue above, and rich
Preference Red on the door —
to create a very special
and individual design.

SPLIT COLOUR

The feature wall has fallen out of favour somewhat and the use of a split colour, or tideline, has taken its place. This is an effect that I really encourage, as there are so many practical benefits to a two-tone wall – and it also looks wonderful.

For example, if you paint a stronger colour on the bottom part of the wall and a lighter colour above, your room will open out and appear bigger, particularly when it is a long, thin corridor. For the ultimate tideline, carry the split colour over and around doors and windows. Be wary of using a strong colour on the top part of the wall, as it can make you feel as if the wall is tipping in towards you and the space is closing in.

To maintain a dramatic effect with a strong colour on the wall, use the same colour but in reflective Full Gloss on the bottom part and the fantastically flat Estate Emulsion on the top. As well as looking super-stylish, Full Gloss is also very durable, making it perfect for homes where there are small children or a heavy footfall.

FACING PAGE, LEFT
There is something so very comforting about a painted floor; this checkerboard pattern in Stone Blue and School House White instantly transports you back in time. The nostalgia continues with Breakfast Room Green on the lower walls and School House White on the upper walls and ceiling.

FACING PAGE, RIGHT
This surprising combination of colours is certainly courageous and gives an extra decorative twist to a relaxed sitting room. Bamboozle has been taken up the skirting and over the bottom third of the wall and paired with Templeton Pink on the top two thirds. The scheme has also been extended over a door that isn't used, to make it 'disappear'.

ABOVE LEFT
The owner of this house chose to keep all the woodwork in School House White for ease and continuity, so the Card Room Green used on the lower wall has been skilfully taken over the door for a really strong, modern look.

ABOVE RIGHT
The subtle combination of colours in this room is to be applauded. Who would have thought that the pairing of delicate Tailor Tack and simple All White could be so effective? The extra band of Tailor Tack turns a charming scheme into something very special.

142

STAIRCASES

To introduce a little drama, consider painting your staircase in a darker accent colour, which will link all the floors of your house together and create a strong central spine. At the same time, the staircase will take on an almost sculptural quality, which is also grounding.

For a sightly gentler approach, just paint the spindles and leave the string, treads and risers, together with any panelling below the stairs, in the woodwork colour of the rest of the space.

Dark spindles on a staircase, in Tanner's Brown, Studio Green or Railings, in Eggshell, are a modern touch. They will introduce some strong colour without being overwhelming.

FACING PAGE
The intention for this pretty cottage was to keep it as bright as possible, which has been achieved by painting the walls in School House White, with the staircase in Pigeon, a decorative twist that makes everything in the room appear lighter.

ABOVE LEFT
This refined hall, painted in stone-coloured Cord, is as understated as it is elegant. The magic here comes from the use of Mahogany (A) on the beautifully restored staircase spindles, offset by Old White on the treads and risers.

ABOVE RIGHT
Elegant, understated Vert De Terre on the walls is joined by Studio Green on the banister and stair treads to create a grounding spine that runs down through this urban but relaxed town house.

FACING PAGE, ABOVE LEFT
This bathroom is certainly arresting, but Eating Room Red on the underside of the bathtub as well as on the beams means that the scheme is grounded. Elephant's Breath with its warm undertone has been used on the walls and ceiling.

FACING PAGE, ABOVE RIGHT
Calluna, which takes its name from the beautiful heather so prolific across the moors of Scotland, feels soft and tranquil yet strangely sophisticated in this bathroom, the perfect recessive shade to complement the iron bathtub.

FACING PAGE, BELOW LEFT
It takes skill to create such a sophisticated bathroom with only painted surfaces and two colours. Wimborne White on the floorboards and the ingenious lateral panelling matches the sanitaryware, while sumptuous Paean Black, not only on the walls but also on the side of the bathtub, unifies the space.

FACING PAGE, BELOW RIGHT
The star of this delightful bathroom, with its Stone Blue walls and Slipper Satin woodwork and ceiling, is the bathtub painted in Off-Black. Although dark, the colour doesn't overwhelm the scheme, as it is way below the eye line.

ABOVE RIGHT
Ammonite has been used on the huge windows dominating this kitchen/dining room, to complement the marble on the kitchen island. The walls have been painted in alluring Oval Room Blue, while striking Railings has been introduced on the island for extra dramatic effect in the middle of the room.

BELOW RIGHT
If you choose a really strong colour for your kitchen walls, such as vibrant Verdigris Green (A), it is a good idea to reintroduce it on your kitchen island, as here, so that you don't leave all the excitement at the edges of the room.

CENTRAL COLOUR

Bold colour doesn't have to dominate, and combining colour with neutral tones can create striking schemes, as well as helping to change the sense of space in a room.

Using a darker colour in the centre of a room will make everything around it feel lighter and brighter. This technique is particularly successful when you paint a central kitchen island in a strong tone. If you don't have an island, you could paint the legs of a table in a darker tone instead, to ground the room, while keeping the strong colour well below eye level. The same can be said of painting the underside of, or the panelling around, a bathtub in a neutral bathroom.

WORKSPACES

If you want to define a work area in a large room, the simplest way is to create a small, individual space within it by using a strong colour on the wall that is as wide as the desk, to give a more intimate feel. To make the space even more enveloping, stop the colour on the wall either at the picture rail, if you have one, or at least 400mm (15in) shy of the ceiling. This will appear to lower the ceiling and create a more intimate zone that encourages concentration as well as promoting a sense of security. Alternatively, repurpose a built-in cupboard by removing the doors and making a desk shelf in the recess. Paint the recess in a strong colour or fun pattern for a vibrant and stimulating workspace.

FACING PAGE

What could be more ingenious than this little flip-down desk built into a recess? And what makes it even more impressive is that the same colour, Stone Blue, has been used on the desk as well as the floor, creating a really seamless scheme. The walls and other woodwork are painted in Shaded White.

RIGHT

There is an engaging element of personal zoning in this room. The fluid shape in Sulking Room Pink, which flows from the wall onto the floor on a background of Light Gray, definitely feels like a claim on the space.

TRANSFORM SPACE WITH COLOUR

LEFT
The height at which tender pink Tailor Tack has been stopped on the walls of this bedroom was dictated by the height of the bed on the other side of the fireplace. Fortuitously, the resulting corner makes the perfect little workspace.

FACING PAGE
Using tongue-and-groove panelling to define a space is a masterful idea, creating a really intimate space in which to work. Painting it in moody India Yellow up to eye level when you are seated at the desk produces the ultimate zoned home office.

RIGHT
If you want to define a space with colour, then you are best off using a really strong one, such as Rangwali. Here, it has been employed to great effect, to make the smallest of workspaces behind some bifold doors. You would never know it was there, but what a delightful surprise it is when you discover it.

FLOORS

There has long been a tradition of painting floors, and suddenly it is very much back in fashion. Floors can be painted in a checkerboard pattern or in stripes, or in a solid colour for a look that is both stylish and practical but always relaxed.

Farrow & Ball Modern Eggshell, our toughest interior finish, covers a multitude of sins, bringing both old and new floors to life. Well-worn floors that have been patched with totally mismatching boards retain their character when painted, while inexpensive new boards gain a slight lustre that lends them a sense of longevity.

Every home contains rooms that would benefit from an easily washable floor covering. However, floor paint should be considered as much for its relaxed decorative qualities as for its durability. As our Modern Eggshell is available in every colour, it is easy to revamp the look of a room by simply painting the floor, and it is a lot less expensive than any other floor covering.

The colour of the floor has a big impact on the look of a room, and the more floor space there is, the greater that impact. A colour used on the floor will always look much lighter than the same tone on the walls, and a pale-coloured floor is the very best way to make the most of any available light. Using a darker colour on the floor than on the walls makes a room look wider, maximizing the feeling of space, so is particularly useful in long, thin halls.

FACING PAGE
This hall floor, painted in Lulworth Blue, brings real cheer to the house that is decorated almost entirely in muted shades of white. The look, which is both pure and humble, brings back the warmth and harmony of a more innocent age.

BELOW LEFT
The occupant of this room has used the aged mushroom colour Dead Salmon on the walls, while painting the floor in lighter Shaded White, like the floors in the rest of the house. The end result is a tranquil but modern-feeling scheme. Having the same colour on all the floors of a home is the perfect way to create a seamless flow.

BELOW RIGHT
Bold Arsenic on the floor of this playroom acts as an anchor and reflects a certain amount of the same shade onto the Pale Powder walls. The mint-green floor is the primary decorative statement in the room, but it doesn't feel overwhelming, as it s[o] far below the eye line — ev[en] if you are very young!

BELOW LEFT

Cheerful and uncomplicated Babouche makes this room feel full of sunshine, and the diamond checkerboard effect on the floor and along the panel of the bathtub has a really striking but somehow friendly effect.

BELOW RIGHT

Another checkered floor but this time on a much bigger scale. Huge painted squares of Beverly and James White are used partly for reasons of design and partly to harness the light flooding through the window and bounce it around the room. In this space, with its Whirlybird walls, a pale-coloured floor is the very best way to make the most of the available light.

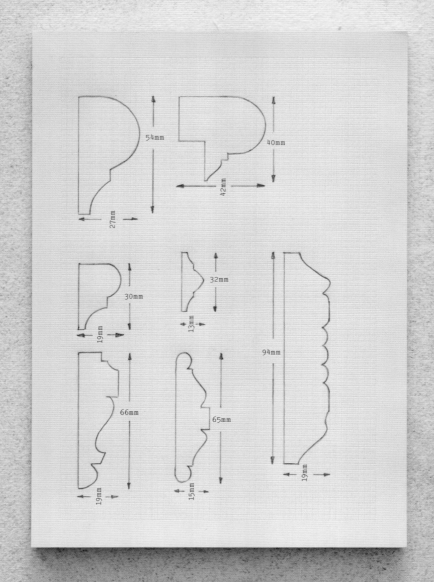

CHAIR AND PICTURE RAILS

It is important to remember that there are no hard-and-fast rules when it comes to decorating picture and chair rails. These architectural elements, and the walls around them, can be treated in many different ways, all of which will have a great effect on the overall appearance of your room.

Picture and chair rails are often painted white through force of habit or, if the mouldings are particularly grand, to draw attention to their architectural beauty. Although there is nothing inherently wrong with this form of decorating, it does tend to create overly busy rooms, because the eye is constantly drawn to the white stripes running around the room, rather than to the beautiful wall colour or the view.

These rails are purely functional parts of the architecture – chair rails protect the walls from furniture, while picture rails are for hanging paintings – so there is no practical reason for them to be picked out in a different colour from the wall. It is only relatively recently that people have attempted to transform them into a feature, giving them misplaced importance and often making them the guiding decorative force.

In most contemporary rooms, the rails are either removed or painted the same colour as the walls for a strong, unified look. As there are no contrasts to distract the eye, the room feels bigger.

FACING PAGE, ABOVE LEFT
Using two such bold colours
in this contemporary
family bathroom is really
heartening. Strong tones,
like Danish Lawn (A) on
the walls and Dinnerware
(A) on the woodwork, go
together so well because
they have the same intensity
of colour, which means that
neither dominates.

FACING PAGE, ABOVE RIGHT
These colours are perfect
for those who are wary of
grey and want to branch out
into colour. Selvedge on the
walls and Hopper Head on
the panelling sit seamlessly
together for the most
cohesive of schemes.

FACING PAGE, BELOW LEFT
Heavenly Stirabout on the
walls will create a glow
in any room. Here, teamed
with historic plaster colour
Templeton Pink on the dado,
it feels particularly warm
and nurturing. This form of
decorating, with a stronger
colour sitting below a
lighter one, will always make
a space feel bigger.

FACING PAGE, BELOW RIGHT
I sometimes worry about
having a strong colour like
Babouche on the walls above a
white dado, in case it makes
the space feel as if it is
tipping in on itself. But the
introduction of a stripe in
this hall creates a balanced,
irresistible, fun-filled
scheme, which feels fresh and
interesting with All White on
the dado and woodwork.

ABOVE
Using two colourways of our
beautiful Hornbeam design
(shown here in BP 5002 and
BP 5004) above and below the
dado rail creates a cohesive
scheme with added interest.

CHAIR RAILS

If you decide to pick out your chair rails and make a feature of them, it is best to do so with the same white (or other colour) that you have used for the rest of the trim. Alternatively, you could try a tone that is sympathetic to the wall colour for a more harmonious visual balance. Simplest of all is to paint over them in the wall colour to make them 'disappear'.

And, of course, having a chair rail gives you the opportunity to consider a range of options for the walls: two sympathetic paint colours, a combination of paint and wallpaper, or two different wallpapers – one above and one below the rail.

Again, there are no rules about which area should be lighter or darker, but using a stronger colour above the chair rail than below can create a feeling of the walls tipping in towards you and the room closing in. Using a darker colour below the chair rail grounds the room and tends to make it open up and feel bigger. This is especially useful in long, thin entrance halls, where a darker colour below the chair rail and a lighter colour on the walls will immediately make the space feel wider and airier.

Farrow & Ball makes combining paint colours and wallpaper especially easy. You can take the background or pattern colour of the wallpaper and paint this below the chair rail, with the corresponding paper above, or vice versa. In this case, it may be best to paint the chair rail the same colour as the wall below, to prevent the eye from being drawn to a white dividing line.

THIS PAGE
I come back to this
tantalizing colour mix
time and time again,
interpreting it in a myriad
of ways: Inchyra Blue on
the dado, Pale Powder on the
upper walls and Preference
Red on the skirting. Heaven!

PICTURE RAILS

There are a number of useful visual tricks that can be played with picture rails to change the appearance of a space.

If the picture rail and the area of wall above it are painted the same colour as the rest of the wall, the ceiling will appear much higher. On the other hand, if the wall colour stops at the picture rail, the eye will be deceived into thinking that that is where the wall ends and the ceiling begins, giving the impression that the ceiling is lower than it really is – a useful device in making a very tall room appear less intimidating.

Another option to consider is to use gradations in colour, where the wall and picture rail are painted the strongest colour, with a slightly lighter version above the picture rail and a sympathetic white on the cornice. This approach opens up a room, making it feel lighter and more spacious.

FACING PAGE, LEFT

It would be challenging to take the maximalist design of our large-pattern wallpaper Heleborus (BP 5606) — here, in a bespoke background colour and James White for the pattern — over the picture rail in this room, as the frieze is so small. Instead, a contrasting colour, Mouse's Back, has been used, capturing the same spirit of nature and making the room feel super-relaxed.

FACING PAGE, RIGHT

The combination of the organic woven pattern of Amime (BP 4405) and our uniquely tactile printing method gives this wallpaper an alluring depth. Here, in Off-Black and Stiffkey Blue, it has been taken up to the picture rail, with Wimborne White on the trim, ceiling and frieze, resulting in a classic, formal look.

ABOVE

Hegemone (BP 5705) wallpaper, with its jolly Vardo background and Churlish Green pattern, is the epitome of joyful decorating. The wallpaper has been taken over the picture rail to increase the perceived height of the ceiling.

ABOVE LEFT

The extraordinary subtle
tones in gentle Eddy are at
their most beautiful when
painted in our Dead Flat
finish. This whole room is
drenched in the one colour,
taken up and over the picture
rail, a technique much
favoured by those who prefer
their rooms to be as calm
as possible, making it ideal
for a nursery.

ABOVE RIGHT

This is bold decorating,
resulting in a wonderfully
vibrant space. Using
Templeton Pink above the
picture rail of a room
painted in Beverly intensifies
both colours, so that the
walls appear greener and
the frieze pinker.

FACING PAGE

There is something so
pleasingly simple about
this design. Rich blue Wine
Dark on the panelling below
Strong White walls makes
the perceived height of the
ceiling drop and the space
feel more intimate.

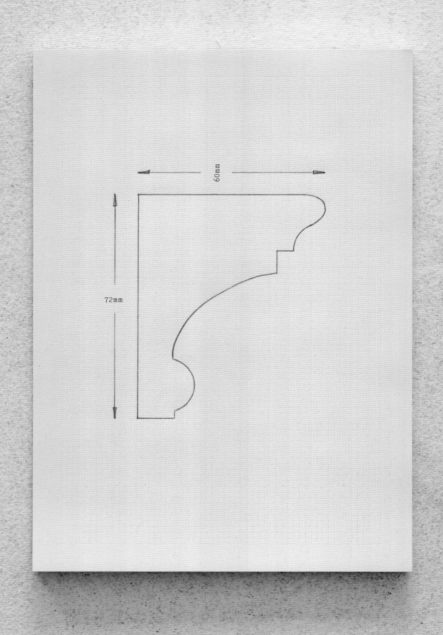

60mm

72mm

CORNICES

Who could imagine that a seemingly insignificant piece of plaster moulding could change the shape, height and style of a room to such a degree? Most people don't give these architectural mouldings much thought, but they can completely transform a space if painted the appropriate colour.

First, I should point out that the mouldings have different names on either side of the Atlantic. In Britain, we refer to them as cornice, or coving, while in the US they are usually called crown moulding. Whichever term you use, I am referring to the decorative element that runs around the top of a room to cover the transition from wall to ceiling.

Embellished cornices tend to be found in larger, more ornate interiors and are to be treasured. The plainer type are generally used in simpler, contemporary homes. However, both can be painted in four basic ways:

Moulding and ceiling the same colour.
Gradating colour from walls to ceiling.
Moulding and walls the same colour.
Pick out the moulding in an accent colour.

MOULDING AND CEILING THE SAME COLOUR

Very often the moulding and ceiling are painted the same plain white, either out of habit or a wish for clean simplicity. However, this does tend to make the perceived height of the room drop by the depth of the moulding. This is because we register the top of the wall at the point where it meets the white of the moulding, making the wall appear shorter than it actually is. Matching the moulding and ceiling is most appropriate when the protruding part of the moulding, which sits on the ceiling, is bigger than the dropping part, which sits against the wall. In this case, it would look clumsy to have anything but the ceiling colour on the moulding.

It is best to paint intricate cornices as infrequently as possible, to prevent the detailing from becoming clogged up with paint. Our Soft Distemper finish is best for detailed interior plasterwork.

ABOVE
In this high-ceilinged room in Oval Room Blue, Wimborne White on both the cornice and ceiling makes the most of the striking detailing.

FACING PAGE, ABOVE LEFT
This intricate cornice, painted in Strong White in a Soft Distemper finish, is partnered with Tailor Tack on the walls, Selvedge on the panelling and Pavilion Gray on the woodwork.

FACING PAGE, ABOVE RIGHT
Chalky, neutral Clunch (A) looks suitably soft when contrasted with Suffield

Green (A) in this house, where the architectural detail makes it impossible to pick out the cornice from the ceiling. Using the same colours on the doors and frames gives a cohesive look.

FACING PAGE, BELOW LEFT
Manor House Gray on the walls and All White on the cornice and ceiling produce a totally classic look.

FACING PAGE, BELOW RIGHT
The contrast between Chinese Blue (A) on the walls and Pointing on the cornice and ceiling creates a dynamic feel in this sitting room.

FACING PAGE
Although this moulding
extends onto the ceiling,
it has been painted the same
colour as the wall. This
works only because James
White on the ceiling is
perfectly complementary
to Lime White on the walls.

LEFT
An ageless combination of
modest grey-green Mizzle
on the walls of this hall
gradates into Lime White
on the cornice and Slipper
Satin on the ceiling, each
colour slightly lighter than
the previous one as they
rise, blending perfectly.

MOULDING AND WALLS THE SAME COLOUR

Painting the moulding the same colour as the walls will make the walls appear taller and the room feel loftier. This approach is particularly effective with plain convex moulding that is used purely as a means to soften the transition from wall to ceiling. Using the same colour on the walls and mouldings also gives a simple and strong, contemporary feel to a room.

GRADATING COLOUR FROM WALLS TO CEILING

To draw attention to your moulding, use a subtle gradation of colour between the walls and the ceiling, thereby creating a visual balance in the room. With a very strong colour on the walls, it may feel uncomfortable to use the same tone on the moulding. In this case, it is best to consider a gradation of colour. Not only will this make the room feel higher, but the eye will be led gently upwards, rather than being pulled dramatically towards the ceiling. Don't forget that for every Farrow & Ball colour, there is a complementary white (see pages 96–7), which can ease the transition between wall and ceiling and contribute to the harmony of a room.

LEFT

Ornate decoration, like on the ceiling at Inchyra House, requires subtle colours, and our Traditional Neutrals feel suitably historic on this fabulous ceiling. Old White, the darkest shade in this group, is used for the background of the moulding, with Lime White on the ceiling and a combination of Off-White and Slipper Satin on the plasterwork.

FACING PAGE, LEFT

Pale, fresh green Palm (A), used here on the walls, has a desaturated quality, as if it is always being seen in a clear, bright light. Perfectly paired with Arsenic on the coving, the look is crisp and captivating.

FACING PAGE, RIGHT

Although there isn't a real cornice in this room, a band of Bancha has been taken around the top of the Yeabridge Green walls in a fun, modern interpretation of traditional decorating.

PICK OUT THE MOULDING IN AN ACCENT COLOUR

It tends to be only the very adventurous who take up the option of painting mouldings in a strong colour. Doing so creates a sharp contrast between the wall and the ceiling, resulting in you constantly reading the shape and confines of the room, which makes the space feel smaller overall.

This method of decoration is most often used when one wants to draw the eye to both the decorative moulding and a ceiling rose, which are best painted in the same colour.

All too often, decorative mouldings, including ceiling roses, have been painted over so many times that they end up losing a lot of their delicate detail. To prevent this from happening and to create an authentic look, use a specialist finish such as our Soft Distemper. Available in a range of colours, its exquisite, soft powdery finish is perfect for very detailed interior plasterwork. Make sure that you check the product details for its suitability in your home, and bear in mind that the moulding must not have been previously painted with an emulsion paint.

CEILINGS

Very little thought tends to be given to the colour of the humble ceiling, but the choice you make will have a huge effect on the overall feel of a room. Consider the ceiling to be your fifth wall and give it due consideration.

Although ceilings are so often painted in some ubiquitous colourless paint, there is no rule to say that they have to be white; in the past few years, the fashion for painting ceilings the same colour as walls has exploded with the realization that most people don't want the size and shape of their room to be defined by the ceiling.

Your ceiling colour can make a room look lighter or darker as well as change the perceived height of the ceiling. And don't forget that Full Gloss on the ceiling has an amazing effect on a room, as does wallpaper – if you are feeling very brave.

FACING PAGE
The colour of your ceiling
is vitally important — it
can set the tone for the
whole house, as it does here.
Painted in Raw Tomatillo
against Au Lait walls and
contrasted with Liquorice
on the door, all of which
makes for the most playful
of homes.

LEFT
This room feels remarkably relaxed. Even though the ceiling has been painted in Wimborne White, it is a shade away from a pure white and complements the Mizzle on the walls. Had the ceiling been painted a bright white, the harmony would be lost.

FACING PAGE, ABOVE LEFT
Taking the Bamboozle wall colour over the ceiling might seem reckless, but such adventurous decorating cannot fail to make you smile. Surprisingly, you are much less aware of the ceiling colour when you are actually in the room.

FACING PAGE, ABOVE RIGHT
I love to use the same colour on walls and ceiling in a bedroom, to prevent my obsessing, while in bed, over the line where colours change. The plaster tones of Templeton Pink create a beautifully tender room.

FACING PAGE, BELOW LEFT
Flamboyant Vardo on the walls and ceiling in this height-restricted space makes for an exciting, enveloping room. Using one colour makes it hard to read where the walls end and the ceiling begins.

FACING PAGE, BELOW RIGHT
Using Suffield Green (A) on the walls and ceiling makes the room's connection with the garden feel almost seamless, creating a lovely, botanical atmosphere.

MAKING A ROOM LOOK LIGHTER OR DARKER

Most of us have grown up with the fixed notion that it is better to make a ceiling as light and bright as possible. However, using a bright white on the ceiling can make a room feel considerably darker. This may sound counterintuitive, but it isn't if you remember that decorating with colour is all about contrast.

The lighter the colour on the ceiling, the darker the walls will appear. A bright white will make even the subtlest of colours feel relatively dark. To prevent this, it is advisable to use a white that is complementary to the wall colour, resulting in a lighter, more cohesive room. To help you choose the best whites to accompany each colour, see pages 96–7.

FACING PAGE

Every surface in the bedroom in this sensational chalet has been painted Dead Salmon, a subtle shade of aged pink with a magical quality that makes it change dramatically according to the light conditions. Here, it creates a subtle and serene environment during the day, becoming super-cosy at night.

BELOW LEFT

The architectural lines in this living area have been softened with the use of Old White on all the surfaces. A colour that you could never tire of, Old White has a discreet grey—green undertone, which gives the fins spanning this building a restrained air, while making you less aware of the sloping ceiling.

BELOW CENTRE

Gentle Pink Ground on both walls and ceiling seems the perfect choice to make this pretty space feel bigger and lighter. If the ceiling was painted white, the walls would appear darker.

BELOW RIGHT

Although one might be wary of creating a feeling of claustrophobia by painting the ceiling in such a strong colour, it is the perfect solution for this slightly compromised space. Wine Dark covers both the walls and the ceiling, making it difficult to read the confines of the room.

SAME COLOUR FOR CEILING AND WALLS

Having the same colour on the ceiling as on the walls creates a soothing atmosphere, and the overall look is much more subtle than you might imagine. With both planes painted in the same colour, it is difficult to tell where the walls end and the ceiling begins, which makes the ceiling appear higher than it really is.

This is particularly effective when there is no cornice and you don't wish to draw attention to the point where the walls and ceiling meet. A continuous field of colour covers up a multitude of sins, and you can camouflage an oddly angled ceiling by taking the colour up the wall and over the ceiling.

CHANGING A ROOM'S PERCEIVED HEIGHT

If you use a bright white on the ceiling of a room with coloured walls, the contrast between the two is so great that one's eye is immediately drawn upwards, to read where the wall ends and the ceiling begins. Having read the top edge of the walls, you are immediately aware of the ceiling height, which causes it to drop.

If, however, you choose a white for the ceiling that is more sympathetic to the tone on the walls, it will feel as if the wall colour has just gradated into a lighter tone on the ceiling. You are then much less aware of where the walls end and the ceiling begins, which means that the perceived ceiling height will rise. Old-school decorators would very often mix 25 per cent of the wall colour into the ceiling white to achieve this effect. Luckily, Farrow & Ball have done all this work for you – there is a complementary white, with the correct coloured undertone, for every wall colour in our palette (see pages 96–7).

It is also worth noting that if you have a very high ceiling and want to bring it down to a more comfortable height, then you should use a darker tone on the ceiling than on the walls. This will visually lower the height of a space and make it more intimate.

FACING PAGE, ABOVE LEFT
Despite the lack of picture rail in this room, Wine Dark has been stopped shy of the ceiling with Kittiwake, which continues to the cornice, creating a stylish gradation to the Strong White ceiling.

FACING PAGE, ABOVE RIGHT
Skimming Stone, a warm, light grey, has been used on the ceiling of this bedroom instead of a conventional bright white, which feels more sympathetic to the Templeton Pink walls and Tanner's Brown skirting.

FACING PAGE, BELOW
Although we often advise using the same colour on the walls and ceiling in such awkwardly shaped rooms, here the combination of All White on the ceiling, echoing the colour of the tiles, and clean Kittiwake on the walls is fresh and uplifting.

RIGHT
Confining the Stone Blue on the walls to between the top of the skirting and the relatively low picture rail makes this room feel more intimate because the ceiling height appears lower.

DECORATIVE CEILINGS

Using colour on the ceiling has recently become increasingly popular. It will create a focal point, particularly in an otherwise neutral scheme, and shouldn't be restricted to just the obvious blue or, indeed, to paint. When entering a neutral room with a coloured ceiling, it takes a moment before you become aware of it, introducing an element of surprise. Even the merest wash of colour on the ceiling will infuse a space with a little individuality.

Subtle colours like Tailor Tack or Cabbage White are a light and charming alternative to white, while adding a decorative twist, particularly in bedrooms and bathrooms.

A strong colour on the ceiling will create an intimate space, especially if it is brought down onto the top of the wall.

Ceilings, whether plaster or panelling, painted in Full Gloss not only have a delightful old world glamour but reflect all the natural light and bounce it around the space.

Using wallpaper on a ceiling might feel too adventurous, however adding pattern will bring excitement to virtually any room. Decorative ceilings have a long history in both architecture and interior design but adding a statement ceiling wallpaper right now feels both fresh and unexpected.

FACING PAGE, LEFT

Although this room in Templeton House was renovated only a few years ago, it feels as if it has remained unchanged for years. Old White, the darkest of our Traditional Neutrals, is used on the walls, with Lime White and Slipper Satin on the ceiling and plasterwork, and Off-White on the trim.

FACING PAGE, RIGHT

The graphic design in this room cleverly incorporates the ceiling above the bed. Painted in rich Brinjal, it helps to create a cosy bedroom.

RIGHT

Creating surprises is just about my favourite way of decorating. In this kitchen rich, olive Bancha has been used on both the walls and ceiling. The twist is that the walls are painted in Modern Emulsion for extra durability and the ceiling is painted in Full Gloss to bounce the light around, as well as to spread some joy.

THIS PAGE
Charlotte created this fun-
filled room for her children
using School House White
Modern Emulsion on the walls
and ceiling, together with
Pink Drab (A) stripes. Oval
Room Blue Modern Eggshell
on both the floor and the bed
ensures extra durability.

CHILDREN'S BEDROOMS

The decoration of children's bedrooms is often the source of considerable angst; the age-old dilemma of whether to keep to the established and timeless colour-flow of the rest of the house or to indulge a child with their choice of colours will never go away. There are, however, many ways around it. Over the next few pages, we cover some understated and practical solutions, as well as some that are more adventurous.

You may want to introduce some extra colour in the form of a feature wall, but this can totally ruin the proportions of a room. Instead, consider using a stronger colour from the bottom of the skirting, up to around 1.2m (4ft) on the walls, and a lighter colour above. This will open out the room and make it look bigger but it will remain cosy for those who may still play on the floor, creating a look that is super-stylish and equally durable. For a really fun look, carry the colour over the doors and windows, or use reflective Full Gloss on the bottom and flatter Modern Emulsion on the top.

Use a strong colour on woodwork and a lighter tone on the walls. Choose a neutral colour sympathetic to your established colour palette for the walls, and then indulge in some bold colour for the skirting and doors. Hague Blue woodwork with Blackened walls is the perfect scheme for the modern child, or swap Blackened for Skylight for a more classic look, evocative of the seaside.

All children's schemes can be enhanced by introducing a bold colour on storage units, beds or other furniture. It's the same as when using a strong colour on a central kitchen island: by placing a darker object in a room, everything around it will look lighter.

BELOW LEFT
Lively Verdigris Green (A)
is the perfect backdrop for
this very special den. It is
made all the more upbeat by
its contrast with Snow White
(A) on the trim.

BELOW RIGHT
You may think at first glance
that this room is painted
totally in School House
White — but look again. A low
border of Treron has been
used to create a snuggly
reading corner.

FACING PAGE
Sunny Yellow Ground is the
perfect backdrop for this
charming mural depicting
characters from the world
of folk and fairy tales.
It has been used on all the
painted surfaces in the
room so as not to detract
from the 'stars' of the show.

If you prefer to keep the walls of your children's rooms neutral in line with the rest of the house, then restricting a stronger hue to a recess or the interior of cupboards or bookshelves is most effective. You can let your child choose this colour which can, of course, be changed easily as they grow in age and sophistication.

Fun wallpaper lining a cupboard is another discreet touch. Bold designs include Closet Stripe and Tented Stripe, while the more delicate Yukutori, with its soft outline of birds, and charming Bumble Bee, a Farrow & Ball favourite, are equally appealing.

Full Gloss on ceilings makes them glint and shine, creating a jewel-like quality. Alternatively, paper the ceiling. The metallic patterns of Brockhampton Star or Vermicelli will catch the light and create a twinkling treat overhead.

Painted stripes, either horizontal or vertical, are a great favourite for ceilings with children of all ages. When created in bold colours, such as Bamboozle and Stone Blue, they have a graphic quality more suited to teenagers. But if you prefer a calmer and more tranquil look, paint stripes in sympathetic neutrals or even in the same colour as the walls but using a different finish.

However you introduce colour or, even if you would prefer a stylish but more subdued room for your child, it will be fun for both of you to be involved in the process. Many children have an inventive and idiosyncratic approach to using colour, which helps to create spaces that reflect their personality and individuality. And, hopefully, you can sign them up early to be a lifelong Farrow & Ball fan.

THIS PAGE
Simple and modern, this is
the perfect interpretation
of a contemporary nursery.
Dusty pink Peignoir has been
used on the walls, but only
up to where they meet the
sloping ceiling of fresh All
White. Treating the walls in
this way makes the ceiling
appear lower. It also has
the added benefit of making
the room feel more intimate,
as well as establishing a
strong graphic look. To add
depth, vibrant Rangwali
covers the floor and skirting.

FACING PAGE

Pink Ground, used on the walls in this nursery, has a yellow base, which gives the paint that very special, plaster-type look and stops the colour from ever appearing sweet and sugary. In this south-facing room, it positively glows.

BELOW LEFT

This is the perfect example of how you don't need to paint children's rooms in strong colours in order to create a jolly atmosphere. The introduction of Selvedge on the floor and Middleton Pink on the cupboard does the job for you.

BELOW CENTRE

Clean, cool blue Kittiwake will remain truly blue in almost any light. It is perfect for a child's room, especially when combined with plant life and natural finishes, such as the sawn wood panelling on the wall seen here.

BELOW RIGHT

If you are keen to use grey, the hint of magenta in Elephant's Breath creates a warmth that makes it perfect for a nursery. It also works especially well with the brilliant white that is so often found on children's furniture.

THIS PAGE
I love how the minimal
contrast between the Parma
Gray background colour
and the Skylight pattern
in the Helleborus (BP 5604)
wallpaper makes its
maximalist design feel
almost subtle. But there
is nothing subtle about the
cheeky choice of Charlotte's
Locks for the peg rail.

WALLPAPER

Choosing wallpaper is extremely personal. Whether you want to make a big, bold statement or just create a little texture on the wall, Farrow & Ball has a wallpaper to suit.

Although most wallpapers are made with ink, ours are not. We use our own paint to create the print, as well as the background colour, using traditional block or trough methods. This results in totally unique papers that work perfectly with our paint colours.

Our huge range of designs is inspired by archives of fabrics and wallpapers from around the world. There are florals, damasks, stripes and geometric patterns, some of which are large and flamboyant, such as Helleborus, while others, like Jasmine are quietly subtle. There should be something for everyone.

In order to make these wallpapers appropriate for use in the modern home, endless work has gone into ensuring that they are wipeable, while still having the same chalky finish that has always defined our paint colours – a combination of timeless artistry and 21st-century durability.

If you are tempted to break into pattern but wary of the commitment, remember to start small – the interiors of cupboards and small bathrooms are crying out for wallpaper. Or use a flamboyant pattern in a room that isn't frequented every day, perhaps a dining room or a guest bedroom. You will be in for a real treat when you do use these spaces, or even just catch a glimpse of fabulous pattern as you pass by an open door.

BIG PATTERN VERSUS SMALL PATTERN

As with so many things in decorating, it seems counterintuitive that a large pattern used in a small space will create the illusion of volume, and a small pattern will have a more enclosing effect, but they do. As a result, wallpapers can be used to great effect to change the shape of a room. Intricately patterned wallpaper, such as Samphire, will immediately make a room feel cosy, while bigger, bolder patterns, such as Tessella, will lend a sense of grandeur and appear to enlarge a space.

FACING PAGE
The delicate stems of Feather
Grass (BP 5107) wallpaper,
with its Green Blue
background and Light Gray
pattern, give an organic feel
with the impression of gentle
movement in the breeze. The
split above and below the
dado rail is truly inspired.

BELOW LEFT
Sweeping Oval Room Blue
blooms on an elegant Pointing
background make for one of
our most popular wallpapers.
The design of this Art
Nouveau inspired Lotus
wallpaper (in BP 2053) brings
a touch of 19th-century
elegance to any kind of home.

BELOW RIGHT
Silvergate, an English
damask (BP 803), was the
first wallpaper made by
Farrow & Ball and it has
certainly stood the test
of time. Always luxurious,
it has an almost velvety
feel, which is something
peculiar to our wallpapers

because they are created
with our own paint. It looks
charming here, with its
pattern in Joa's White and
background in Pointing.

DAMASKS

Farrow & Ball have always been famous for their damasks. The smaller patterns of Brocade and Renaissance are perfect when combined with paint in either their background or pattern colour – usually the paint below the dado rail and the paper above. The larger damasks, like the stunningly pretty French damask St Antoine and its simpler English counterpart Silvergate, together with the more graphic Orangerie, make big statements when used in strong colours, while in their more neutral colour combinations, the pattern becomes much less obvious. This is also true of Lotus, where the strong colourways are as popular with those looking to make a grand statement as the neutral colourways are with those wanting the subtlest of patterns.

THIS PAGE
Although this Arcade (BP 5307) wallpaper was inspired by the Art Deco designs of the 1940s, it feels particularly modern in this urban, minimalist kitchen. The beauty of using a Farrow & Ball wallpaper is that you can have complete confidence there will be paint colours to go with it. Studio Green, the colour of the pattern, has been painted on the doors, creating a totally seamless design.

FACING PAGE

What could be more engaging
than using the woven pattern
of Amime (BP 4404) in two
different colourways: Off-
Black and Dix Blue below the
picture rail, and a bespoke
colourway on the frieze? Both
wallpapers are shown to best
effect by the traditional
woodwork in Cornforth White.

BELOW LEFT

Tessella (BP 3603), with its
Arsenic pattern, looks its
very best here, combined
with Moroccan tiles on the
skirting. Contemporary and
confident, it makes a bold
geometric statement but
never overwhelms, because
you see so much more of the
background than the pattern.

BELOW RIGHT

Our Bumble Bee (BP 555) paper
has long been a favourite
for bedrooms and bathrooms,
but in stronger colour
combinations, such as this
bespoke colourway with gold,
it lends itself to all parts
of the home. The bold painted
dado line in Pitch Black here
ties in with the metal doors.

PLAYING WITH SCALE

Mesmerizing Enigma, with its interlocking rectangles, makes a grand statement, as does Tessella, but on closer examination it is the slightly raised texture, a result of our traditional printing method, that really brings these wallpapers to life.

Many Farrow & Ball papers tend to break up the wall, preventing it from appearing too flat, rather than creating a pattern. Blostma and Vermicelli are both excellent at doing this, while the diminutive patterns in Polka Square and Yukutori almost disappear at a distance but bring hidden delights close-up. These are complemented by the slightly bolder Lattice and Amime, both of which can be hung vertically or horizontally. Brockhampton Star is the prettiest and most traditional of papers and can be used on both walls and ceilings. The timeless, effortlessly versatile and wildly popular Bumble Bee cannot fail to make you smile.

BELOW LEFT

We all want to bolster our connection with nature, and what better way than using the stylized motif of cloud-pruned hornbeams in this wallpaper? Here, Hornbeam (BP 5007), with a Stiffkey Blue background and a Dix Blue and Wimborne White pattern, sits above Wimborne White panelling to create a room that seems to cross the boundaries of both modern and traditional.

BELOW RIGHT

The outsized pattern of Helleborus (BP 5605) wallpaper in the most vibrant of background colours, Vardo, creates an incredibly stylish room, where the furniture has been chosen to match the walls for additional impact.

FLORALS

Sumptuous Peony, Wisteria and Hegemone are big, blowsy patterns. With their touch of the botanical, they are wonderful for introducing a garden-like feel to a large room. The more delicate patterns of Uppark and Jasmine, both of which can be taken onto the ceiling, will do the same for a smaller room. Charming Feuille has the simplicity of an original woodblock, perfect for those wanting a mid-century feel, while Hornbeam, with its stylized motif of cloud-pruned trees, is modern and light-hearted, as are the organic-feeling Bamboo and Atacama, with its tropical design of cacti. The outsized patterns of Helleborus and Feather Grass are perfect for making a grand statement on a feature wall.

Although yellow rooms fell out of favour for quite some time, the amazing sunny quality that yellow can bring to a space has once again been recognized. And what could be more joyful than this Helleborus (BP 5607) wallpaper, in a bespoke background colour with a Pointing pattern, which makes the room feel luminous even on the darkest of winter days?

The flowing floral pattern of Hegemone (BP 5701) always feels optimistic. This interpretation, using colours from our Relaxed Neutrals group — Purbeck Stone for the background and Cornforth White for the pattern — is no different. The wallpaper sits perfectly with Ammonite on the ceiling and woodwork.

FACING PAGE

This wallpaper, simply named Stripe, is a fresh take on a true classic. Here it is hung horizontally, making it look more contemporary, between Raw Tomatillo shutters, the colour of which is echoed in the paper alongside Hog Plum and Au Lait for an extremely exciting but seamless look.

BELOW LEFT

At a mere 19mm (¾in) wide, Closet Stripe is our slimmest stripe, which brings a classic look to traditional spaces. However, if you hang the design horizontally, it immediately looks more contemporary, as shown with this archived paper in a seaside bathroom.

BELOW CENTRE

Since our Plain Stripe (ST 1172) wallpaper is created using a traditional 19th-century technique, you can see how the stripe colour is layered onto the background. This gives it a really unique appearance, whether the colour combination is a light neutral or a moody dark, as in this sitting room.

BELOW RIGHT

A combination of four colours is used in each of our five Chromatic Stripe wallpapers, all of which make an adventurous design statement. This colourway (BP 4203) includes Terre d'Egypte and Mahogany (A). Offcuts have been used on the chair – but I wouldn't advise siting on it!

STRIPES

Farrow & Ball stripes come in many shapes and sizes and are enduringly popular. They are, however, all timelessly elegant, from the classic one-colour Plain Stripe and its wider version Broad Stripe to the more graphic Chromatic Stripe, made up of four colours. For those who want a little more pattern in their stripes, Tented Stripe and Block Print Stripe offer an extra twist and work as well in children's rooms as they do in traditional studies. Because of their neutral backgrounds, Closet Stripe and Five Over Stripe are perfect for those craving a fresh, uncomplicated feel. All stripes can be hung vertically, in the more traditional way, or horizontally, to create a more unusual space. No matter how they are used, our stripes always appear smart and classic.

BELOW LEFT
The heritage design of our delightful Rosslyn (BP 1925) wallpaper has been brought right up to date with the introduction of gold to the pattern, against the deep, warm tones of Charleston Gray in the background.

BELOW RIGHT
Glamorous Lotus (BP 2071) wallpaper has always caused a stir but here, with its copper design and De Nimes background, it stops you in your tracks. Totally stunning!

BOTTOM LEFT
The juxtaposition of gold against the background of rich Stiffkey Blue in this Yukutori (BP 4307) wallpaper is the ultimate in chic and perfect for creating excitement in a small space or on a feature wall.

BOTTOM RIGHT
The vertical nature of our Bamboo (BP 2161) paper always helps to make rooms feel loftier. The Sulking Room Pink background and gold pattern echo the linear wood panelling and complement the rich tones of the wood floor.

METALLICS

We have expanded our wallpaper collection with a selection of covetable metallic prints, bringing some of our best-loved designs to life with striking shades of gold, silver and copper. From charming Gable and simple Yukutori to glamorous Tourbillon and hypnotic Enigma, these wallpapers are amazingly tactile and will add a touch of drama and luxury to any room with their subtly shimmering finish. Who doesn't want a bit of shine in their lives?

ABOVE LEFT
The interlocking rectangles of our Enigma (BP 5509) wallpaper look particularly arresting in gold against a Paean Black background. Any natural light reacts with the metallic pattern and bounces around the room.

ABOVE RIGHT
I simply cannot resist this wallpaper pattern, and have used it in different colourways in cupboards throughout my house. The intricate botanical design of Atacama (BP 5807), shown here in Stiffkey Blue and bespoke silver, never fails to bring a smile to my face.

ABOUT OUR WALLPAPERS

There are three very important points to be made about our traditionally made and beautiful wallpapers:

1. They are printed with genuine Farrow & Ball paints, so will work seamlessly with walls, ceilings and woodwork painted in colours from our palette.
2. They are recyclable at the end of their life because they are printed onto responsibly sourced, vinyl-free paper with our own water-based paint.
3. Each roll is finished with a fine layer of specially formulated glaze, which ensures that the paper is wipeable and as durable as it is beautiful.

EXTERIORS

Exterior colour not only makes a property appealing from the street, it also sets the tone for the whole house. All of the exterior – masonry, walls, window frames, ironwork, planters and the front door – may need to be painted and should be considered as a whole, just as you would the architectural elements in a room.

Colour used outside can have a truly transformative effect. Whether you want to complement pale honeyed stonework with modest shades, disguise a house clad in weatherboarding or make a stunning backdrop for plants and foliage, don't forget to always work with the architectural elements as well as with nature. The colour of guttering or drainpipes should be chosen to complement the lead on a building, just as the colour of a bench under a fabulous blossom tree should be selected to enhance the shade of the flowers.

As with interiors, when it comes to choosing colours, there are no rights or wrongs, but it is best to take into account certain factors such as the location of your property, as described on the following pages.

FACING PAGE
With the use of thatch becoming increasingly rare, it is a pleasure to see this charming cottage sympathetically painted in Wimborne White Exterior Masonry paint, together with soft Pigeon Exterior Eggshell to create some definition on the woodwork.

CONSIDERING YOUR SETTING

When decorating the exterior of your home, you can afford to consider a shade that is darker than a colour you might choose for the interior, because the light conditions are so different. If, for example, you are considering Shadow White for the outside based on how it looks indoors, try the stronger Drop Cloth, or Templeton Pink instead of Setting Plaster.

Choose colours that suit the environment, and always look at possible colours in situ. Vibrant tones that might seem perfect in the bright sunshine of the Caribbean may look too strong in a northern light. Similarly, the subtle tones of a crofter's cottage will appear lifeless in bright sunshine.

Dominant features like brickwork, natural wood and other expanses of colours, such as paved or gravelled areas, lawns, fencing, shrubs and even flowers, should also be taken into account, as they all affect colour choice.

In a rural setting, you may want the house to recede into the landscape. In this case, muted, green-based tones, such as Old White or Lime White, work best on masonry, with sympathetic Slipper Satin on the woodwork to minimize contrasts. For a mellow, sophisticated look, paint any planters and benches positioned against the house in one of the many 'stone' colours: Oxford Stone for a warm look, Fawn (A) for a greener feel, or String for an understated, yellower scheme.

In an urban setting, it is more important to be sensitive to the style and colour of neighbouring buildings, and decide whether you want to have a complementary or contrasting scheme. If the entire street has white trim, it may be wise to follow suit – even the subtlest off-white could look dirty against bright white on an adjacent building. For this reason, strong colours like Hopper Head and Beverly are now popular on exterior trim because they stand out from the crowd.

TREATING THE ENTRANCE

The eye will always look for a focal point, and you can always use colour to help you make one. To make a feature of your home's entrance, paint the front door and its entire frame in one colour, which will make it look bigger and more imposing. And if you have a porch, consider taking the same colour over the walls and ceiling for added drama. When you pass through this darker area, it will make everything inside look bigger and lighter.

It is a good idea to paint the front door and any neighbouring woodwork, such as garage doors, window boxes and garden gates, in the same colour.

There are two finishes to choose from: Full Gloss on the door, for gravitas, and the slightly less formal-looking Exterior Eggshell on everything else. Exterior Eggshell, with its low sheen level, creates a relaxed feel in soft colours, and a more contemporary look in strong colours. Full Gloss, meanwhile, gives a classic, more traditional look and is especially effective in strong colours, which look both chic and discreet.

ABOVE RIGHT
What a treat for passers-by to see the juxtaposition of Green Smoke and Eating Room Red on the exteriors of these historic houses.

BELOW RIGHT
Ammonite Exterior Masonry paint on the walls and Pigeon Exterior Eggshell on the front door of this country house could not feel more at home. Note how the door colour has been painted around the arch as well, to make the door look bigger.

FACING PAGE
The dark, uncertain tones of Inchyra Blue, originally created to reflect the moody Scottish skies, look almost mid-tone on this door bathed in sunlight. It is amazing to see how much paler all colours look when seen in natural light.

FACING PAGE AND THIS PAGE
These seven front doors of very different styles have been painted in an assortment of colours and finishes. Stone Blue Exterior Eggshell (far left) looks charming with the shutter painted to match, while deep, warm pink Crimson Red (A) (left), also in Exterior Eggshell, certainly brings some personality to this house. A front door painted in Pitch Black Full Gloss (right) will always have a certain grandeur, while Railings in Exterior Eggshell (below right) looks that little bit more relaxed. Neutral or white front doors have become extremely popular again and this is a great example, painted in Shaded White Exterior Eggshell (below). What could be more chic than the front door of this London town house painted in Deep Reddish Brown (A) Full Gloss (below left) or more convivial than the stable door in Serge (A) Exterior Eggshell (below far left). Each has its own merits, but which one suits you?

CONNECTING INTERIOR AND EXTERIOR

Using the same colour on the exterior and interior of a house creates a seamless continuity and often makes the rooms feel bigger. Take the wall colour of a room, however vibrant, and use it on a flowerpot or bench in the garden, to visually connect the two spaces. If the same colour is chosen for both exterior and interior window frames, this helps to blur the distinction between the house and garden. And if the window frames are also painted the same colour as the walls, you will instantly feel more connected to your outside space.

When it comes to garden tables and chairs, you need to decide whether you would prefer them to be a bold feature or a subtle part of the garden. Soft colours with an organic feel, such as Treron or Pigeon, will sit seamlessly on garden chairs or the legs of a garden table, to merge into the landscape for a very natural look. But if you prefer to reflect the colours of your planting in your garden furniture, Brassica and Cinder Rose – colours inspired by nature – are firm favourites outside and are often used in combination with soft greens like Vert De Terre.

ABOVE LEFT
Wildly romantic Cinder Rose on this wooden garden furniture sits easily on the patio and feels totally at one with nature.

ABOVE RIGHT
Dix Blue contains a large dose of green and, with its vintage feel, makes a great choice for garden furniture. The French-style iron table and chairs look utterly charming among the greenery.

ABOVE LEFT
Green Smoke was chosen specifically for this garden room, to echo the tones of the verdant landscape, which it does very successfully. Painting all the surfaces in one colour really makes you feel that you are a part of the outdoors.

BELOW LEFT
The layers of our green-grey family in this room — Eddy on the walls and ceiling, French Gray on the window reveal, and Treron, the darkest tone, on the shutter — create an instant connection with the exterior through the outsized window.

215

ABOVE
French Gray woodwork and
a Railings front door, both
in Exterior Eggshell, could
not be more classic. They
look both handsome and
refined on the outside of this
impressive country house.

FACING PAGE, LEFT
This gorgeous garden pavilion
is painted in Shaded White
Exterior Eggshell. The colour
takes its name from the soft
tone created when white is
used in deep shade. Here, in
bright sunlight, it looks
suitably elegant.

ABOVE, RIGHT
Even the most diminutive
of buildings need careful
consideration when it comes
to colour. The warm tones of
Joa's White on this playhouse
look completely at home in
the dappled light.

THE PERIOD OF YOUR PROPERTY

The architectural style of your property, and the period in which it was built, is more relevant when it comes to painting the exterior of your home than the interior. Elegant Regency houses need only neutrals on their stucco facades and equally understated colour on their front doors, while Victorian houses can definitely sustain stronger colours.

The colour families outlined in the Neutrals section of this book (see pages 76–91) can be layered on exteriors, to enhance or detract from the architecture, just as you would do in an interior. However, do not use more than three colours on the exterior, otherwise it will start to look messy.

THE
DIRECTORY

COLOUR COMBINATIONS

The joy of the Farrow & Ball palette is that there are endless colour combinations at your fingertips. Of course, colours look quite different depending on the light conditions and where they are used, but the following combinations, chosen purely because they are my personal favourites, have been tried and tested in a huge range of properties worldwide. Each group creates wonderful spaces, whether subtle and understated or thrillingly dynamic. I hope there will be something here to appeal to everyone.

Lime White
Old White
Blue Gray

Sometimes you just have to go back to the original and the best! Lime White was the first colour in the Farrow & Ball palette, and when it is joined by its equally soft partner Old White and the timeless tones of Blue Gray, it results in decorative schemes that feel as if they have been there forever.

Pink Ground
Setting Plaster
Templeton Pink

The tender blushing tones of Pink Ground and Setting Plaster have recently been joined by the slightly stronger Templeton Pink, all of which are just right for creating the perfect sanctuary in our busy modern world. For the ultimate in subtle design, use Templeton Pink on the trim, Setting Plaster on the walls and Pink Ground on the ceiling.

Selvedge
Calke Green
Bone

This scheme sums up the very essence of the current approach to decorating. A mix of traditional and contemporary colours, which has become a firm favourite of mine, it creates spaces that feel dynamic but not overwhelming. These colours can be used in any combination but I favour Calke Green walls, Bone trim, and Selvedge cabinetry.

Bamboozle
Beverly
Jitney

Inspired by the deeply saturated colours of 18th-century merchants' houses, the colours in this strong combination have become extremely popular. They could be painted on all the surfaces in interconnecting rooms, or fiery Bamboozle and deep green Beverly could be used on trim, to complement walls in comforting Jitney.

Eddy
French Gray
Treron

A simple scheme of these closely coloured layers will create the peaceful environment we all seem to crave at the moment. Their strong affinity with nature makes them particularly suited to garden rooms. Use them in any combination on trim, walls and ceilings – and feel your shoulders drop.

Red Earth
Stirabout
Tanner's Brown

These classic harmonious colours, each with roots in the past, are a sublime combination that perfectly showcases our return to earthier colours in the home. The terracotta tones of Red Earth on the walls are at their best when combined with deep rich Tanner's Brown on the trim and the delightfully warm Stirabout on the ceiling, for a look that is truly warm and comforting.

Light Blue
Hague Blue
Picture Gallery Red

You may well have spotted something very similar to this fantastically popular combination in the book already! Sophisticated Hague Blue feels somewhat more approachable alongside Light Blue, and these colours are often both used on the same walls, with the stronger tone below and the lighter one above. The scheme is all the more enchanting when Picture Gallery Red is introduced on the doors or windows.

Sap Green (A)
Pink Cup (A)
Bancha

This combination is a guilty pleasure of mine and always enjoyed by my guests. Although Farrow & Ball is famous for its sophisticated, muted palette, sometimes we just crave colours that simply make us smile. Try Sap Green (A) on the walls, with slightly stronger Bancha on the trim, topped off with a Pink Cup (A) ceiling. Go on, I dare you!

Tailor Tack
Pale Powder
Skimming Stone

This scheme is all about being light and breezy, and is ideal if you are decorating the rooms off a small hall and want them to have their own identity, while maintaining a perfect balance and flow. Magical Skimming Stone, a warm grey, is the perfect foil on hall walls for adjacent rooms painted in delicate Tailor Tack and Pale Powder, a gentle shade of aqua.

Dead Salmon
Preference Red
Shadow White

This combination is one way of interpreting the use of warmer tones, but with a strong, 'old school' feel. One of my favourite schemes for very small rooms is to use Dead Salmon on the trim and 1m (3ft) up the wall, with Shadow White on the upper walls and ceiling. The introduction of a band of Preference Red between the two makes it even more chic.

Hopper Head
Wine Dark
Borrowed Light

Rooms painted in darks such as these may not be for the fainthearted but they do result in fabulous spaces to retire to at night, defining the end of your working day. A TV room or snug with walls and trim painted in rich Wine Dark feels good for the soul, while a floor in Hopper Head will set it off perfectly. Use Borrowed Light in Full Gloss for an extra design twist.

Green Smoke
Planter (A)
Pantalon (A)

There is something delightfully informal about this enduringly popular group of colours. Somehow they always seem familiar and rarely pose a challenge, due to the weathered nature of their slightly sombre tones. Particularly suited to exteriors, they can be used on garden furniture, as well as on outdoor trim, for a stylish but understated look.

OUR FINISH FINDER

Finishes	Tin Size Available	Approximate Coverage* (m²)	Sheen %	Usage
Our most matt finish, with added toughness, for interior walls, woodwork and metal				
Dead Flat	750ml	9	2	Walls, ceilings, woodwork and metal
	2.5 litres	30	2	
	5 litres	60	2	
Our super-tough, washable, interior modern finishes are great for kitchens and bathrooms				
Modern Emulsion	2.5 litres	30	7	Walls and ceilings
	5 litres	60	7	
Modern Eggshell	750ml	9	40	Wood, metal and concrete, including interior floors
	2.5 litres	30	40	
	5 litres	60	40	
Our Estate range gives you the signature Farrow & Ball look in two low-sheen, interior finishes				
Estate Emulsion	100ml	1	2	Walls and ceilings
	2.5 litres	35	2	
	5 litres	70	2	
Estate Eggshell	750ml	9	20	Wood and metal
	2.5 litres	30	20	
	5 litres	60	20	
Our durable, weather-resistant finishes				
Full Gloss	750ml	9	95	Interior/exterior wood and metal
	2.5 litres	30	95	
Exterior Eggshell	750ml	10	20	Wood and metal
	2.5 litres	32	20	
Exterior Masonry	5 litres	40	2	Brick and render
Our traditional finishes bring an authentic touch to historic properties and features				
Casein Distemper	2.5 litres	32	2	Interior plaster walls and ceilings
	5 litres	65	2	
Soft Distemper	5 litres	65	2	Interior detailed plasterwork
Limewash	5 litres	Varies on conditions	2	Interior/exterior. Professional application advised

All our colours are available in our Dead Flat, Modern and Estate finishes. To check the colour range of our other finishes, visit farrow-ball.com

SEQUENCING YOUR DECORATING

———

How should you start your decorating? Some people like to choose their paint colours first, but this can make life a lot more complicated when everything else in your home has to work with them. Better to start with the less flexible elements, such as flooring, and then use our wonderfully comprehensive colour card to find a complementary tone.

We would suggest looking at the different elements of your home in the following order:

Flooring: Carpet, wood or tiles have a huge influence on the overall look of your design.

Kitchen and bathroom worktops: Due to long lead times, kitchen and bathroom units are often the first things you have to choose colours for, so it makes sense to have already chosen your worktops to avoid any colour clashes.

Fabrics: Give yourself time to select fabrics you love without having to match them to wall colours you have already chosen.

Walls and trim: Now it's time for glorious colour and wallpaper! Spend time with our colour card and wallpaper patterns. Remember to test the colours in your home, as described on pages 92–3. Alternatively, have a Farrow & Ball Colour Consultant come to help you in your home.

Consider how the light affects the rooms in your home (see also pages 42–7). South-facing rooms (in the northern hemisphere) will be lighter than those facing north, and colours in east- or west-facing rooms will change dramatically through the day. If you use certain spaces primarily at night, they might benefit from richer tones, while daytime spaces often suit being light and bright.

One key decision to make is to work out if you are happy for the woodwork/trim colour to change from room to room, or whether you would prefer to have just one tone running throughout the house.

Begin by thinking about the colour of your hall. Would you like it to be as light and spacious as possible, or would you prefer something stronger that will make the rooms off it appear lighter? It is also important to consider the sightlines from room to room at this point. The hall colour can unify the house.

List every element you need to decorate. Remember that the colour of the trim/woodwork can be as important as that on the walls, and that all these elements have to work together.

Analyse the room and how you use it. Do you want to make it look longer, squarer, higher, lower? Should it be intimate in feel, or fresh or calm. This can all be achieved with paint colour. Small spaces, guest rooms or a rarely used dining room might give you an opportunity to be more adventurous with colour and pattern – you probably spend little time in such rooms, and any guests who use them will be made to feel extra special.

A Farrow & Ball colour fan is a great investment when choosing colours. You can remove the pages of the colours that interest you and stick them on to the wall, to sample them in situ, and also carry them with you when choosing fabrics and flooring. Alternatively, you can buy sample paint pots.

When you have chosen your colours, don't forget to select the correct paint finishes. Good luck with your decorating!

PREVIOUS PAGE
Wine Dark, with its deep blue, spiritual feel, makes this sitting room feel really intimate. It is combined with heather-like Calluna on the floor — a surprising choice that makes the space feel even cosier, as does the use of Wine Dark on both the walls and trim.

FACING PAGE
One of the joys of Studio Green is how it responds to different light conditions. In a room flooded with natural light, it looks obviously green, but in a darker space, such as here, it becomes really intense, creating a velvety surface that is very close to black.

ARCHIVE

At Farrow & Ball, we have always believed in keeping an easy-to-use curated palette. Although we love to make new colours, our colour card has never featured any more than the 132 we feel will most appeal to the current market.

When new colours are developed, it is with a heavy heart that we have to retire some still much-loved paint shades. Fake Tan, Monkey Puzzle, Pea Green and Biscuit are just a few of the archived but still greatly treasured Farrow & Ball colours.

All our wonderful, limited-edition collections are included in the Archive, the latest being the California Collection, a palette of eight, sun-soaked paint colours, along with our Colour by Nature collection, where all the colours are taken from the exact hues and corresponding parts of animals, vegetables and minerals from across the natural world. Never fear, even though these colours are less visible in our showrooms, they can easily be ordered in any finish from the factory, where the original recipes are kept safely in our archives. A lot of people consider these colours to be hidden gems.

Many old favourites have been the inspiration for new colours. They've just been subtly changed to suit the contemporary home. But if you still love an original colour, whether Broccoli Brown or Fruit Fool, they are readily available from our website.

As mentioned previously, all archive colours in this book have been marked with (A).

ABOVE RIGHT
Ash Grey (A) in this understated sitting room has a relaxed feel that makes it suited to any space. The underlying green in this shade means that it appears more intensely coloured in natural light and greyer in areas of low light.

BELOW RIGHT
The pairing of Pantalon (A) on the units and Berrington Blue (A) on the wall works perfectly, as they both have large doses of black in their undertone. In spite of this, the kitchen featured here could not have a friendlier, more modern atmosphere.

The esoterically named
Skimmed Milk White (A),
with its extraordinary
softness, creates the perfect
backdrop for rich, earthy
Olive (A) on the door and
light strip in this modish
hall. This is audacious
decorating at its best.

THIS PAGE
Every great decorator
reveres their brushes.
As with this group, they
become more than just tools
and more like old friends.

HOW TO PAINT

———

Doing the decorating yourself can feel a little overwhelming, but the following tips, together with an outline of essential items (see pages 230–1) and our Finish Finder (see page 222), should make the job a little easier. You are about to transform your home, and the process should be fun.

- Clear as much as you can from the room or cover it with dust sheets. Use masking tape around the edges of the trim, sockets and carpet to protect it from the wall colour.
- Gather your tools and materials together. You will need a stick to stir your paint, to ensure it is properly mixed, and some good-quality brushes and rollers. Keep a damp cloth or rag to hand to mop up any spills.
- Professional painters will always spend more time prepping than actually painting. Loose paint and plaster need to be removed by a scraper or sandpaper. When covering previously painted trim, you should lightly sand the surface to create a key for the paint to bond to.
- Clean your entire working area to make sure it is completely free of dust and dirt.
- Do not skip the priming or undercoating stage, however tempting that might be. Priming is designed to stabilize surfaces and prepare them for the paint and will significantly help the coverage and application of your topcoat.
- Now comes the fun bit: the painting. Stir the paint in the tin for a few minutes, to make sure it is mixed well, and then decant it into your paint kettle and roller tray.

- Start with the ceiling. Cut into* where the ceiling meets the wall, usually with a 50mm (2in) brush. Using the roller and pole, start rolling evenly across the ceiling area, overlapping by 50 per cent as you go. When the first coat is dry, repeat the process. You will always need to apply two coats (for every surface).
- Next, paint the walls. Cut into the edge where the wall meets the ceiling without touching the finished ceiling colour. Some practice may be needed to get this line straight, so be patient. Cut into all the wall edges, architraves and skirtings. Take care to apply the paint evenly, as a thicker edge may show through the finished paint.
- Finally, paint the trim or woodwork. With your Wood Primer & Undercoat and weapons of choice, usually a 25mm (1in) or 50mm (2in) brush, start to cut into the windows, doorframes, doors and, finally, the skirtings, making sure you don't go onto your finished walls. Follow this with two topcoats. Always do your skirtings last. These are the areas that may pick up dust and this avoids transferring it to other, more noticeable areas.
- Keep a record of the colours and finishes you have used in case you need to touch up any areas in the future. Store any leftover paint in a cool, dry place, protected from frost and extreme temperatures.

*	Cut into: using a brush to paint areas a roller cannot reach or where a neat edge is required.

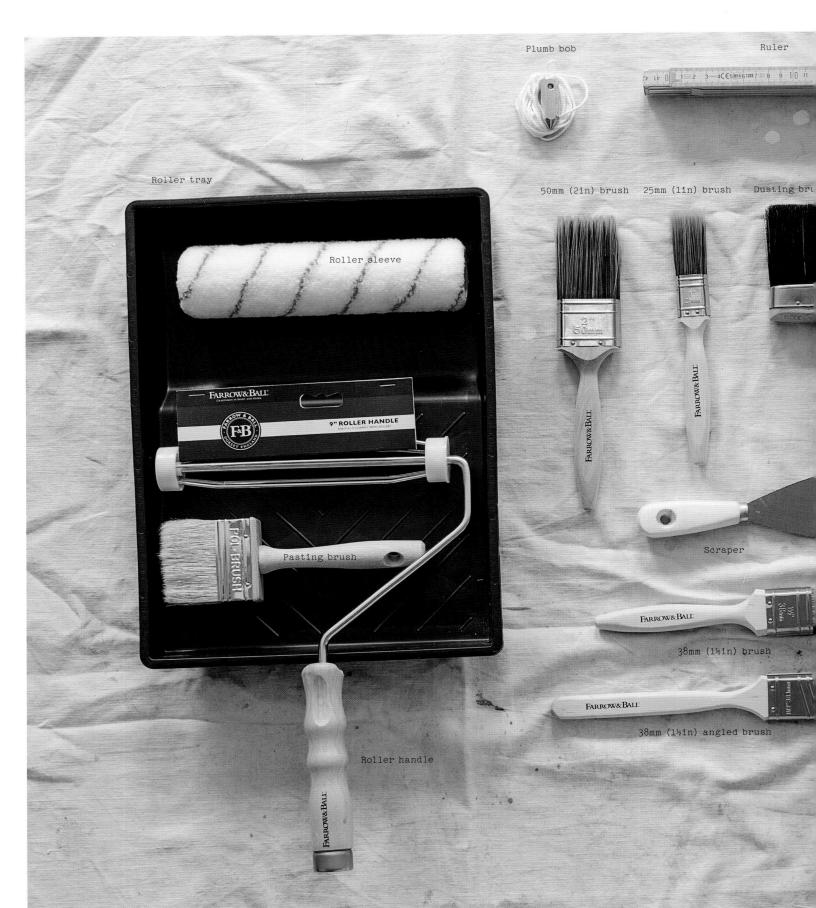

Plumb bob

Ruler

Roller tray

50mm (2in) brush   25mm (1in) brush   Dusting bru

Roller sleeve

FARROW&BALL
CRAFTSMAN IN PAINT AND PAPER

F&B
FARROW & BALL
DORSET ENGLAND

9" ROLLER HANDLE
FOR 9" x 1.5" (22MM x 38MM) ROLLERS

Scraper

POT BRUSH

Pasting brush

FARROW&BALL   1½" 38mm

38mm (1½in) brush

FARROW&BALL

FARROW&BALL

FARROW&BALL

38mm (1½in) angled brush

Roller handle

Paper-hanging brush

Paint kettle

Masking tape

Blades

Snap knife

Filling knife

Tape measure

Wallpaper scissors

Pasting brush

Decorator's sponge

Dust sheet

PAINT FINISHES

———

Our comprehensive range of paint finishes offer different practical benefits. They can easily be divided into four key groups, as explained below. It is worth noting that not all finishes are available in all markets.

- Unless you are doing specialist decorating, there is really only a choice of three finishes for walls:
  Estate Emulsion or the equally beautiful but more durable
  Modern Emulsion and
  Dead Flat, with its ultra-matt finish.

- You have a choice of four finishes for woodwork, although these can also be used on walls and ceilings:
  Estate Eggshell
  Modern Eggshell
  Dead Flat
  Full Gloss

- When it comes to painting outside, these exterior finishes can be used for walls as well as woodwork:
  Exterior Masonry
  Exterior Eggshell
  Full Gloss

- And for specialist decorating, there are the following:
  Limewash
  Casein Distemper
  Soft Distemper

Whichever finish you choose, you are safe in the knowledge that our interior and exterior paint finishes are water-based, low-odour, quick-drying and toy safe (see also pages 252–3). Learn more about the finishes themselves and how they can be used on the following pages.

FACING PAGE
The fabulous light in this dining area has been enhanced by the use of soft School House White on the walls and ceiling in super-flat Estate Emulsion, which gives the walls an almost velvety appearance. Stone Blue on the sideboard is fresh and fun, but does not overwhelm the purposefully neutral scheme.

RIGHT
Both the Yeabridge Green walls and the Bancha border in this room have been painted in Estate Emulsion, so they react beautifully to the changing light conditions throughout the day.

ESTATE EMULSION

The distinctive chalky and very matt finish of our Estate Emulsion makes it a classic paint finish for low-traffic interior walls and ceilings. As well as minimizing any imperfections, it creates a beautiful depth of colour.

LEFT
Some might question the use of Great White for the walls of a room where logs are stacked, but the Modern Emulsion finish makes it super-durable. The light colour flatters the warm tones of the other finishes.

FACING PAGE
The owner of this family kitchen has chosen to dispense with a splashback, depending instead on the wipeable qualities of our Modern Emulsion finish, which repels steam as well as spills. Templeton Pink on the wall complements the Setting Plaster units, painted in Modern Eggshell.

MODERN EMULSION

Our super-tough finish for interior walls and ceilings is washable, scuff-proof and protects against mould. Available in our full range of colours in a beautiful matt finish, Modern Emulsion is suitable for every room in the home, and is the best choice for kitchens and bathrooms.

LEFT
The view into this bathroom from the living space of a beautifully designed shepherd's hut cannot fail to make the heart sing. All the surfaces outside the bathroom have been painted in lively Stone Blue Estate Eggshell. The combination of this and intense Cane (A) Estate Eggshell on the small cupboard sitting against School House White walls is totally captivating.

BELOW LEFT
This familiar setting,
where the original version
of this book was written, has
recently been redecorated
with Stirabout Estate
Emulsion on the walls and
rich Beverly Estate Eggshell
on the window frames, in
order to form a connection
with the trees outside.

BELOW RIGHT
This simple panelling has
been painted in easy-going
Faded Terracotta (A) Estate
Eggshell. Soft and warm,
it characterizes the earthy
colours recently welcomed
so avidly into our homes.
It sits seamlessly with
natural Light Sand (A)
Modern Emulsion on the walls.

ESTATE EGGSHELL

This washable, water-based satin finish is for using on interior
wood and metal, its soft, low-shine finish bringing an understated
elegance to trim and furniture. It is suitable for doors, radiators
and other wood and metalwork throughout the home.

MODERN EGGSHELL

With its mid-sheen finish, Modern Eggshell is our toughest interior finish, adding colour and protection to wood, metal and concrete surfaces. This ultra-durable eggshell is tough enough for floors, and it can also be used throughout the home on skirting, doors, kitchen cabinets, furniture and radiators.

ABOVE LEFT
This room manages to be both elegant and relaxed with its pared-back combination of Shaded White Estate Emulsion on the walls and De Nimes Estate Eggshell on the door. No doubt the calm atmosphere is reinforced by the use of Modern Eggshell, also in Shaded White, on the floor.

ABOVE RIGHT
What joy to open this kitchen cupboard, painted in charming Stirabout, to reveal spicy Bamboozle, both in Modern Eggshell, on the inside! Stirabout Modern Emulsion has also been used on the walls.

ABOVE

This wood-clad chalet is
full of wonderfully muted
Farrow & Ball colours,
such as Dead Salmon in
the bedroom. They all sit
seamlessly together, but
a cheeky little twist has
been added to the Oval
Room Blue bathroom, with
the use of India Yellow
on the underside of the
bathtub. All the finishes
are Modern Eggshell.

FACING PAGE
What could be more
spectacular than this hall
drenched in Stiffkey Blue?
The walls, ceiling, ornate
cornicing and woodwork have
all been painted in the
same Dead Flat finish, not
only creating a super-stylish
space but also making the
decorator very happy!

RIGHT
This room embraces two of
the biggest trends of the
moment: using the same colour
on every surface and making
sure that it is a seriously
warm one. Red Earth in this
space ticks all the boxes.

DEAD FLAT

An extraordinarily matt finish with added toughness, Dead Flat is
multi-surface and suitable for interior walls, woodwork and metal,
including radiators. Washable, wipeable and scuff-resistant, Dead
Flat creates incredibly rich colours that also last.

FULL GLOSS

If you want a high-shine finish, Full Gloss is an ultra-high-gloss,
water-based finish suitable for both interior and exterior wood
and metal. It brings a touch of glamour to walls and ceilings, as
well as being resistant to water, flaking, peeling and fading for up
to six years when applied in line with our Product Advice Sheets.

LEFT
De Nimes is an elegant blue that feels wonderfully down to earth but at the same time always fashionable. Used in Exterior Eggshell on the front door of this handsome house, it grounds the building while remaining understated, sitting quietly with the simple All White window frames, also in Exterior Eggshell.

FACING PAGE, ABOVE RIGHT
This charming garden gate and fence have been painted in Pantalon (A) Exterior Eggshell. The colour has a mysterious tone that is neither brown nor green, so it works in combination with the planting throughout the seasons, making it the perfect choice here.

FACING PAGE, BELOW LEFT
Deep olive Bancha never fails to thrill. Used in Exterior Eggshell on the walls of this outside bathroom, it introduces a botanical touch in keeping with the setting.

FACING PAGE, BELOW RIGHT
The walls of this London town house in Lulworth Blue Exterior Masonry paint have a really friendly feel about them — a happy colour to welcome you home! The front door painted in classic Down Pipe Exterior Eggshell adds an element of sophistication.

EXTERIOR MASONRY

For brick, render and concrete, Exterior Masonry is our super-matt, long-lasting finish for exterior walls. Its water-resistant formula protects walls, while offering the highest level of water vapour permeability, which allows them to breathe. Applied in line with our Product Advice Sheets, it resists flaking, peeling and fading for up to 15 years.

EXTERIOR EGGSHELL

For a low shine finish on exterior wood and metal, Exterior Eggshell brings long-lasting colour to outdoor spaces with a finish that remains flexible once dry, protecting wood and metal surfaces through changing weather. Added preservatives help to prevent the growth of algae and fungi. Applied in line with our Product Advice Sheets, this resin-rich formula resists flaking, peeling and fading for up to six years.

LIMEWASH

Recommended for a breathable finish and to achieve added texture, historical Limewash is used for interior wall and ceilings as well as exterior walls, where it bonds to the building itself to give protection from the elements. Professional application is recommended.

CASEIN DISTEMPER

This strengthened distemper is for use on low-traffic walls and ceilings. It offers a very flat matt finish with a breathable, permeable structure.

SOFT DISTEMPER

This traditional distemper has an exquisite, soft, powdery finish and is recommended for very detailed interior plasterwork. Its blend of natural resin and minerals means it can be delicately applied, allowing detail to be preserved on intricate mouldings.

FACING PAGE, FAR LEFT
The period panelling in this hall looks particularly special because there is so much 'movement' in the paint colour. In this case, it is down to the application of Drop Cloth by the home owner, but a similar effect can be achieved with the use of Limewash on the walls.

FACING PAGE, LEFT
Fun was had with the walls of this hall: a Light Gray wall was speckled with deep Railings and subtle Ammonite, all in Casein Distemper, to create an effect that appears as if it has always been there.

RIGHT
If you have moulding as special as the one in the sitting room of this elegant home, then it is advisable to paint it in Soft Distemper with its very soft powdery finish, so the ornate design really comes to life. Here, the natural tones of Jitney on walls are complemented by School House White on the cornice and ceiling — simple but effective.

PAINT FINISHES

PRIMERS AND UNDERCOATS

———

Remember that preparation is key to successful decoration. To make certain that you have the most beautiful and long-lasting interiors, all of our colours has a recommended Primer & Undercoat colour, to give you a surface primed for attention in order to achieve a fortified finish. These Primers & Undercoats are formulated with the same ingredients and rich pigments that enhance our topcoats.

Wall & Ceiling Primer & Undercoat
Designed for use under Estate Emulsion and Modern Emulsion, this Primer & Undercoat will achieve an even finish for the topcoat.

Wood Primer & Undercoat
For use on bare or previously painted interior and exterior wood, including floorboards and knots. This Primer & Undercoat creates a smooth, protective, easy-to-paint base for our Eggshells, Full Gloss or Dead Flat, and a durable, colour-rich finish.

Metal Primer & Undercoat
A rust-inhibiting Primer & Undercoat for metal surfaces, including metal gates, railings, furniture, radiators and drainpipes.

Masonry & Plaster Stabilising Primer
For use on interior and exterior masonry, rendered or plastered surfaces that are porous, chalky or slightly degraded but otherwise structurally sound.

ABOVE AND FACING PAGE
The care and artistry that have gone into the decorating of this bedroom and bathroom know no bounds. In the bedroom, the walls were first painted in Cromarty but only up to a certain height, where a shadow effect was created by switching the colour to Blue Gray. Then stripes of Card Room Green were hand-painted over the base. The same technique was used in the bathroom, with All White and Dimpse on the walls and bold Verdigris Green (A) stripes. This decorating shows real dedication — but, wow, it is so worth it.

ENVIRONMENT

From our award-winning responsible practices to recyclable materials, we're committed to reducing our impact on the planet without compromising on quality. By choosing to craft our entire range with a water base using renewable energy, we've already taken steps and we're always looking for more.

100% WATER-BASED RANGE

Since 2010, we've crafted all our paints with a water base, even our Full Gloss and Eggshells. Virtually odourless with low, or even trace, levels of VOCs – meaning no nasty fumes – and rated A+ for indoor air quality*, they're comfortable to apply, easy to live with, and still wonderfully rich in colour. You can also wash them from brushes using only water, with no harsh solvents – especially useful if there are little ones around. And with children in mind, our Dead Flat, Modern and Estate finishes are certified toy-safe** so, you can confidently transform toys, nursery furniture and more.

French Indoor Air Quality Decree N° 2011-321 – Arrêté April 2011
**Safety of Toys Part 3: Migration of certain elements (EN 71-3:2019+A1:2021)*

CRAFTED WITH CONSCIENCE

Our paint and wallpaper are handcrafted in Dorset, a few tins and rolls at a time, using wind and solar power. We only work with people who share our ethos, which includes working with FSC® certified printers, who use FSC® certified paper, to produce our printed items. We also use sustainably sourced paper for our wallpapers and source our rich pigments from responsible suppliers fully compliant with the Modern Slavery Act. We even recycle 100% of waste from our factory, so nothing goes to landfill.

LONG LASTING

A durable paint finish will keep your space fresh for longer, so you won't have to repaint as often. From scrubbable, scuff-resistant Dead Flat to mould-resistant Modern Emulsion for bathrooms and kitchens, and not forgetting our weather-resistant Exterior range, our long-lasting finishes can help reduce your long-term impact. Plus, because our metal tins are infinitely recyclable and our wallpaper is vinyl free, it's possible to recycle empty tins and any offcuts, to further reduce waste going to landfill.

ABOVE LEFT
The geniuses in our paint laboratory have worked for many years to make our most popular finishes toy safe, so they can be used on cots, toys and more. This cot in Parma Gray Modern Eggshell looks perfect against a wall in Suffield Green (A).

ABOVE RIGHT
I love the audacity of using Picture Gallery Red on this wheelbarrow and tool shed — what a boost to your gardening! Although a bold colour, a generous helping of brown pigment deepens the red so that it doesn't feel out of place, even in the fields.

ERAS

——

I f you are nostalgic for the past, you may want to source authentic colours for your home. However, it is a grave mistake to pressurize yourself into using only colours that are historically correct. Better to remember that our homes are to be lived in and enjoyed in the 21st century, regardless of when they were built.

The joy of colour is that it has developed over the years, and we should embrace this, together with the changes that have taken place in our buildings – we now have bigger windows than ever before and definitely better lighting. The Farrow & Ball palette has been designed with this in mind, so the colours seem both ageless and up to the minute. They are perfect interpretations of true period colours.

The pictures on the facing page show the types of colours used in the four main decorative periods.

LEFT
This corner of a reception room in a very special 16th century rural manor feels like a small glimpse into the past. Farrow & Ball paints have been used extensively for the enovation of the property, to give it a suitably historic feel.

GEORGIAN

'Lichen'

'Off-White'

'Mouse's Back'

'Picture Gallery Red'

VICTORIAN

'Citron'

'Joa's White'

'Eating Room Red'

'Parma Gray'

EDWARDIAN

'Ringwold Ground' (A)

'Wimborne White'

'Skylight'

'Cooking Apple Green'

ART DECO & MID-CENTURY

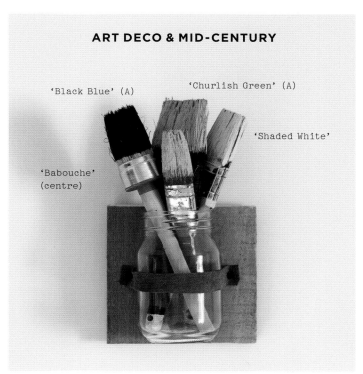

'Black Blue' (A)

'Churlish Green' (A)

'Shaded White'

'Babouche' (centre)

GLOSSARY

Architrave
Moulding around a door or window.

Ceiling rose
Rounded decoration, usually mounted in the centre of the ceiling.

Cornice
A decorative border where the wall meets the ceiling. Sometimes referred to as crown moulding.

Coving
A simple concave border used to eliminate the interior angle between the wall and ceiling.

Dado
The lower part of the wall below the dado/chair rail when decorated differently from the wall above it.

Dado rail/chair rail
A horizontal moulding fixed to an interior wall at around waist height.

Fascia boards
A broad, flat, horizontal board that runs along the lower edge of the roof.

Frieze
The upper part of the wall between the picture rail and the cornice. Or an ornamental band around the top of the wall.

Glazing bars
Slim pieces of timber or metal used to divide a single pane of glass into a series of smaller panes.

Panelling
Wood or plaster panels lining a wall.

Picture rail
A horizontal moulding fixed to an interior wall from which pictures can be hung.

Quoins
Decorative bricks that form the corner of external walls. Sometimes referred to as cornerstones.

Skirting
A border of wood (or occasionally plaster) that is joined to the bottom of an interior wall where it meets the floor to protect it from kicks and dirt. Sometimes referred to as a baseboard.

Tongue and groove
Boards fitted edge to edge to create panelling.

Woodwork/trim
A blanket term for skirting, doors and frames, windows and frames, and any additional joinery.

FARROW & BALL SHOWROOMS

UK

Bath
124–126 Walcot Street
Bath
Somerset
BA1 5BG
+44 (0) 1225 466700

Battersea
146 Northcote Road
Battersea
London
SW11 6RD
+44 (0) 20 7228 6578

Beaconsfield
39 London End
Old Beaconsfield
Buckinghamshire
HP9 2HW
+44 (0) 1494 677700

Blackheath
48 Tranquil Vale
Blackheath
London
SE3 0BD
+44 (0) 20 8852 9836

Bristol
19 Princess Victoria Street
Clifton
Bristol
BS8 4BP
+44 (0) 1179 733900

Cambridge
14 Regent Street
Cambridge
Cambridgeshire
CB2 1DB
+44 (0) 1223 367771

Chelsea
249 Fulham Road
Chelsea
London
SW3 6HY
+44 (0) 20 7351 0273

Cheltenham
15-17 Suffolk Road
Cheltenham
Gloucestershire
GL50 2AF
+44 (0) 1242 230898

Edinburgh
20 North West Circus Place
Stockbridge
Edinburgh
West Lothian
EH3 6SX
+44 (0) 131 226 2216

Esher
15 High Street
Esher
Surrey
KT10 9RL
+44 (0) 1372 477129

Glasgow
470 Great Western Road
Glasgow
G12 8EW
+44 (0) 141 337 7043

Guildford
11 Tunsgate
Guildford
Surrey
GU1 3QT
+44 (0) 1483 511365

Hampstead
58 Rosslyn Hill
Hampstead
London
NW3 1ND
+44 (0) 20 7435 5169

Harrogate
18–22 Albert Street
Harrogate
North Yorkshire
HG1 1JT
+44 (0) 1423 522 552

Henley-on-Thames
21 Thameside
Henley-on-Thames
Oxfordshire
RG9 2LJ
+44 (0) 1491 636128

Hove
31b Western Road
Hove
East Sussex
BN3 1AF
+44 (0) 1273 774640

Islington
38 Cross Street
Islington
London
N1 2BG
+44 (0) 20 7226 2627

Leamington Spa
82 Regent Street
Leamington Spa
Warwickshire
CV32 4NS
+44 (0) 1926 424760

Manchester
270 Deansgate
Manchester
M3 4JB
+44 (0) 161 839 5532

Marylebone
64–65 Paddington Street
Marylebone
London
W1U 4JG
+44 (0) 20 7487 4733

Notting Hill
21–22 Chepstow Corner
Notting Hill
London
W2 4XE
+44 (0) 20 7221 2328

Oxford
225 Banbury Road
Summertown
Oxford
OX2 7HS
+44 (0) 1865 559575

Richmond
30 Hill Rise
Richmond
Surrey
TW10 6UA
+44 (0) 20 8948 7700

Solihull
36 Mill Lane
Mell Square Shopping Centre
Solihull
West Midlands
B91 3BA
+44 (0) 121 709 3360

St Albans
36 Market Place
St Albans
Hertfordshire
AL3 5DG
+44 (0) 1727 847155

Sunningdale
5 Broomhall Buildings
Sunningdale
Surrey
SL5 0DH
+44 (0) 1344 876615

Tunbridge Wells
4 High Street
Tunbridge Wells
Kent
TN1 1UX
+44 (0) 1892 512121

Wilmslow
19 Church Street
Wilmslow
Cheshire
SK9 1AX
+44 (0) 1625 415102

Wimbledon
90 High Street
Wimbledon
London
SW19 5EG
+44 (0) 20 8605 2099

Wimborne
Uddens Estate
Wimborne
Dorset
BH21 7NL
+44 (0) 1202 890905

Winchester
32 The Square
Winchester
Hampshire
SO23 9EX
+44 (0) 1962 843179

EUROPE

Cologne
Pfeilstraße 20
50672 Cologne
GERMANY
+49 22 12 77 36 761

Düsseldorf
Hohe Straße 37
40213 Düsseldorf
GERMANY
+49 21 12 10 73 561

Frankfurt
Kaiserstraße 25
60311 Frankfurt
GERMANY
+49 69 24 24 62 69

Hamburg
Neue ABC-Straße 2–3
20354 Hamburg
GERMANY
+49 40 21 98 22 35

Lyon
24 Cours de la Liberté
69003 Lyon
FRANCE
+33 4 72 32 98 14

Munich
Rumfordstraße 48
80469 Munich
GERMANY
+49 89 21 26 94 16

BHV Rivoli
52, rue de Rivoli
75004 Paris
FRANCE
+33 1 42 74 90 68

Paris Le Chesnay
BHV Parly
Centre Commercial
Parly 2
Le Chesnay
78158 Paris
FRANCE
+33 9 62 69 28 47

Paris Marais
111 Bis Rue de Turenne
75003 Paris
FRANCE
+33 1 44 61 18 22

FARROW & BALL SHOWROOMS

Paris Neuilly
2 rue du Château
Neuilly-sur-Seine
92200 Paris
FRANCE
+33 1 47 22 98 28

Paris Rive Gauche
50 rue de l'Université
75007 Paris
FRANCE
+33 1 45 44 82 20

Paris St Germain en Laye
7 rue du Docteur Timsit
St Germain en Laye
78100 Paris
FRANCE
+33 1 39 10 46 50

Strasbourg
1 rue de la Nuee Bleue
67000 Strasbourg
FRANCE
+33 390 20 08 30

NORTH AMERICA

Berkeley
1813 Fourth Street
Berkeley
CA 94710
USA
+1 510 848 8153

Bethesda Row
7118 Bethesda Row
Bethesda
MD 20814
USA
+1 202 479 6780

Boston
One Design Center Place
Suite 201
Boston
MA 02210
USA
+1 617 345 5344

Brooklyn
383 Atlantic Avenue
Brooklyn
NY 11217
USA
+1 718 858 8840

Chicago
449 North Wells Street
Chicago
IL 60654
USA
+1 312 222 9620

Dallas
1301 Oak Lawn Avenue
Suite 150
Dallas
TX 75207
USA
+1 214 206 8210

Greenwich
32 East Putnam Avenue
Greenwich
CT 06830
USA
+1 203 422 0990

Los Angeles
741 N La Cienega Blvd
West Hollywood
Los Angeles
CA 90069
USA
+1 310 652 6834

NY Flatiron
32 East 22nd Street
New York
NY 10010
USA
+1 212 334 8330

NY Midtown
D&D Building Suite 1519
979 Third Avenue
New York
NY 10022
USA
+1 212 752 5544

NY Upper East Side
1054 Lexington Avenue
New York
NY 10021
+1 212 737 7400

Orange County
3323 Suite C Hyland Avenue
Costa Mesa
CA 92626
USA
+1 714 438 2448

Pasadena
54 West Green Street
Pasadena
CA 91105
USA
+ 626 796 1459

Paramus
160 Route 17 North
Paramus
NJ 07652
USA
+1 201 265 4030

Santa Monica
1016 Montana Avenue
Santa Monica
CA 90403
USA
+1 310 857 5811

Toronto
1128 Yonge Street
Toronto
M4W 2L8
CANADA
+1 416 920 0200

*For the most up-to-date list
of showrooms and stockists,
please visit farrow-ball.com*

INDEX

—

A little pocket of calm to
end on. Our Drag wallpapers,
which are created using a
single colour, look wonderfully
simple – the traditional
application method leaves
beautifully textured
brushmarks on the surface
of the paper. Here, it is
perfection in delicate
Pink Ground (DR 621).

ACKNOWLEDGMENTS

Ten years after writing the original *How to Decorate*, I am thrilled to be thanking pretty much the same group of people again – we got the team back together and what a merry team it is!

So, many, many thanks go to all at Octopus, who expertly guided this now third-time writer through the process of creating this book with as much care as they did the first time. Particular gratitude goes to Alison Starling for her unfailing support, to Jonathan Christie for his thoughtful design and unerring patience, to Polly Poulter for her wise guidance, and to Helen Ridge for her extraordinary diligence.

Once more, a special thanks goes to the wonderfully talented Farrow & Ball team, particularly Joanna Darch for her enormous hard work and commitment while curating the images for this book.

We are obviously indebted to the home owners from all over the world who so generously allowed us to photograph their beautiful properties and include them in this book, and to the wonderful James Merrell who captured them so skilfully with his camera. Thanks also to Robin Kitchin, not only for his major contribution, but for his patience while working with me over the last few years.

I am extremely lucky to still have a job that I am as passionate about now as I was when I started – it is as challenging as it is fun – and much of this is down to my friend and co-worker Charlotte Cosby who, as always, I am indebted to.

This book is dedicated to Cos, Nanc, Bea and Raff, along with those two pairs of indispensable 'hands'!

An Hachette UK Company
www.hachette.co.uk

First published in Great Britain in 2023 by
Mitchell Beazley,
a division of Octopus Publishing Group Ltd,
Carmelite House,
50 Victoria Embankment,
London EC4Y 0DZ
www.octopusbooks.co.uk
www.octopusbooksusa.com

Text and illustrations copyright © Farrow & Ball
Limited 2023

Distributed in the US by Hachette Book Group,
1290 Avenue of the Americas,
4th and 5th Floors,
New York, NY 10104

Distributed in Canada by
Canadian Manda Group
664 Annette St., Toronto, Ontario,
Canada M6S 2C8

ISBN 978-1-78472-899-1

A CIP catalogue record for this book is available
from the British Library.

Printed and bound in China

10 9 8 7 6 5 4 3 2 1

Page 212, top right and bottom right: Photo
by @kensingtonleverne in collaboration with
@Collagerie

Text: Joa Studholme
Photographers: James Merrell, Robin Kitchin,
Boz Gagovski

Publisher: Alison Starling
Creative Director: Jonathan Christie
Senior Editor: Pollyanna Poulter
Copy Editor: Helen Ridge
Proofreader: Julie Brooke
Senior Production Manager: Katherine Hockley

ENDPAPERS
It was a very special moment
when the great colourist
John Sutcliffe, who assisted
Tom Helme in creating the
signature Farrow & Ball
colours, sent me this colour
card. It might be a scrappy
old piece of paper but it
was the start of a colour
phenomenon, and I couldn't
treasure it more.

JOA STUDHOLME

Colour Curator Joa Studholme has worked with Farrow & Ball for more than 25 years and has become a key part of the brand's story. She helped launch the first showroom, became the first Colour Consultant and has created many of the paint colours. As well as introducing new colours, Joa's current role focuses on showing people the power of paint to transform a space. She shares her passion for colour through colour consultancy, her 'Colour in the Home' talks and her books *How to Decorate* and *Recipes for Decorating*. Joa splits her time between London and Somerset and, as to be expected, both her homes are brimming with Farrow & Ball colour. In fact, her love for colour means she is constantly redecorating.

CHARLOTTE COSBY

Creative Director Charlotte Cosby has been working with Farrow & Ball for the past 17 years. She has full responsibility for creative direction, including product development, brand identity, photography, showroom design and much more. Charlotte is passionate about pattern, colour and design, and spends her free time with her family renovating her Victorian home by the sea.

JAMES MERRELL

London-based James Merrell is the book's photographer. James's work has been featured in *W*, *Elle Decor* (all editions), *Vogue Living*, *Town & Country*, *Domino*, *Food & Wine*, *Martha Stewart Living*, *Departures*, *Travel + Leisure*, *The Wall Street Journal* and *Living Etc*. It has also appeared in many bestselling interiors books.

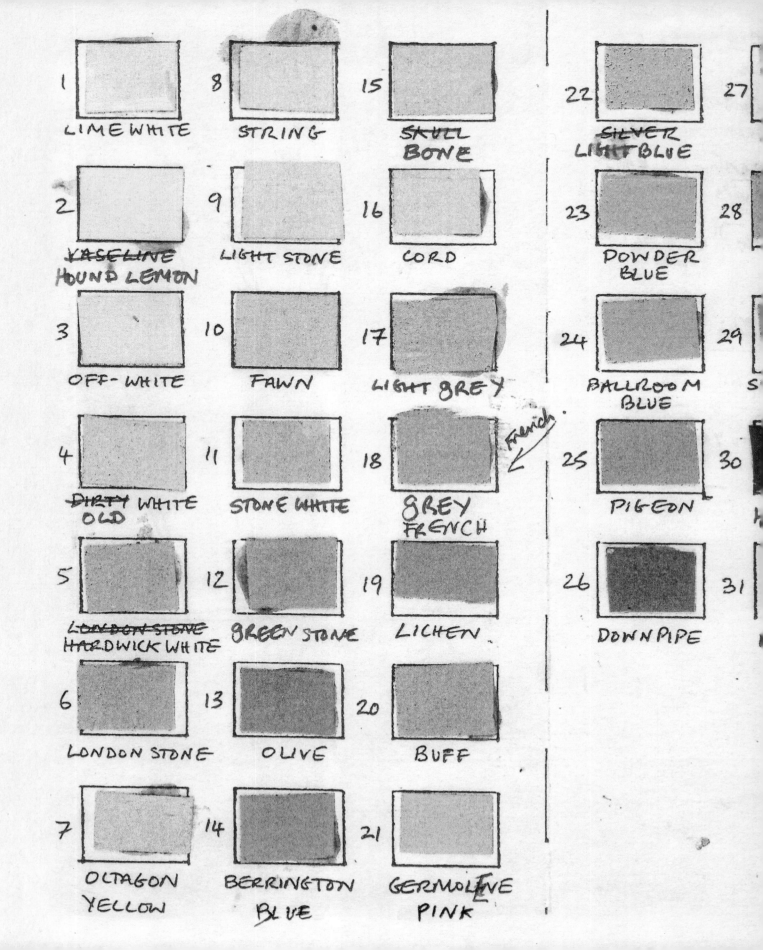

1 LIME WHITE

8 STRING

15 SKULL BONE

22 ~~SILVER~~ LIGHT BLUE

27

2 ~~VASELINE~~ HOUND LEMON

9 LIGHT STONE

16 CORD

23 POWDER BLUE

28

3 OFF-WHITE

10 FAWN

17 LIGHT GREY

24 BALLROOM BLUE

29

French

4 ~~DIRTY~~ OLD WHITE

11 STONE WHITE

18 GREY FRENCH

25 PIGEON

30

5 ~~LONDON STONE~~ HARDWICK WHITE

12 GREEN STONE

19 LICHEN

26 DOWNPIPE

31

6 LONDON STONE

13 OLIVE

20 BUFF

7 OCTAGON YELLOW

14 BERRINGTON BLUE

21 GERMOLENE PINK